*SEARCH*

*Diane Kennedy Pike*

# SEARCH

The Personal Story of a Wilderness Journey

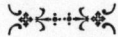

Doubleday & Company, Inc.
Garden City, New York

Copyright © 1969, 1970 by Diane Kennedy Pike
All rights reserved
Printed in the United States of America

to

BISHOP JIM PIKE

*whose search for Truth
is an example and an inspiration
and whom I love*

## TABLE OF CONTENTS

| | |
|---|---:|
| *Foreword* | ix |
| *A Short Drive into the Wilderness* | 1 |
| *If I Die Here* | 17 |
| *The Web of Life* | 33 |
| *Shalom, Shalom* | 45 |
| *Nowhere to Be Found* | 55 |
| *Don't Give Up Hope* | 77 |
| *The Shadow of Death* | 99 |
| *The End of a Search* | 119 |
| *Peace and Joy* | 139 |
| *Monotheistic Marriage* | 157 |
| *A Journey's End* | 171 |
| *No Regrets* | 193 |

# FOREWORD

I had not had any idea how many people across the nation were watching, waiting and praying during those long days while Jim was lost in the desert. The experience was so intense for me that I felt the world must have stopped—but I knew only of the concern of those who communicated directly with me by telegram or phone. Since returning from Israel, however, the large volume of mail from persons all over the country expressing their deep sense of personal loss at Jim's death—though many knew Jim only from afar—and their profound personal involvement in the agony of those days we were searching have helped me appreciate more than ever before what Jim's life meant to hundreds—even thousands—of people both here and abroad.

It was actually at the urging of the Board of Directors of the Bishop Pike Foundation (before Jim's death, the Foundation for Religious Transition), however, that I decided to tell the story in full. They felt all who had followed the events so closely should have an opportunity to know the deep inner meaning it had for Jim and me.

Jim has always been a public figure. It seems appropriate that those events which led to his death should be shared with the large "congregation" of his admirers and followers, with whom he surely would have shared them had he lived to tell the story himself. He spent many years giving of himself openly, hoping to help others find the freedom to open up to new growth too. I hope this book manifests that same style.

The title refers not only to our search for Jim in the desert, but—and more important—to Jim's search for Truth and personal freedom. The two are not, however, unrelated, as I hope the story reveals. The life-style which Jim and I had chosen led us into the desert. If our going there, Jim's dying and my living to tell the story can open a door for any reader to a renewed search for Truth, a tribute will have been paid to my husband—whom I feel was a great man of faith and an example to us all. He was fearless in seeking new understanding, he welcomed new opportunity for growth and he had an unquenchable thirst for knowing the Truth.

The story is told as it actually happened. My first inclination—not being quite as bold as my husband—was to edit out some of the more unesthetically human aspects of it, dwelling more on the emotional and spiritual. But that would have distorted the nature of the experience, which included the transformation of the ordinarily distasteful, painful and even horrible into vehicles for deeply significant insight into the nature of Reality.

I hope the reader will try to enter the experience with me at all levels, recognizing that it is in the midst of our humanity with all its limitations and frailties that God's power and love are given us, making the mundane seem divine. One who sees through eyes of love sees only beauty. I am grateful to have had that experience in my relationship with Jim—and in our wilderness journey. I hope the reader will be able to catch something of what this means to me by sharing the journey set forth here.

I want to extend here my sincere and profound gratitude to the Bethlehem police, who conducted the search

## FOREWORD

for Jim under the leadership of Major Enosh Givati and Chief A Ben Schmauel. Several officers were out on the search every day, as were other members of the police force, and their persistence long after they would ordinarily have given up hope means more to me than I can say. I am also grateful to the many volunteers from the ranks of the Army who went out to search for Jim on their leisure hours, the members of the special border police, one of whom discovered Jim's body that last day, and the civilian volunteers who were members of the Society for the Preservation of Nature. The latter were principally responsible for finding Jim; they went deep into the canyon and found all the clues leading to the discovery of his body.

Special thanks are also due to the management and staff of the Intercontinental Hotel in Jerusalem, whose compassion, understanding, special courtesies and attentive service made those long six days bearable, and to Miss Margaret Barnhart, American consul in Jerusalem, who accompanied me through many long hours of eternal waiting and helped in more ways than I could count.

To my family for their support through all those painful hours of uncertainty—and since then in my grief—there are no words adequate to express my gratitude. Their love for me from the beginning of my life has made everything possible—the deep joy and freedom of my love for Jim, the hope during the search, and the living out of the grief here at home. My life will have to be my thanks to them; I hope it will be adequate.

And gratitude is due all the dozens of friends and family, and the hundreds I knew less well or not at all, who prayed for us during those long hours. Neither Jim nor I could have made it through our wilderness journey without that supportive strength. Special thanks go to our friends John and Ellen Downing, who flew to Israel in time to join us for the committal service, John acting as priest.

For help in preparing this manuscript, I am indebted to Mrs. Gertrude Platt and Mrs. Joyce Duncan, New Focus Foundation secretaries, both of whom have worked with Jim since he first moved to Santa Barbara, have seen him through innumerable crises, both personal and ecclesiastical, and have now stayed loyal to me past his death. To call them merely secretaries would not do justice to the friendship they have shown.

And, finally, my brother Scott. There is no way to say what he has meant. His role in the search is described in the book. He has also shared Jim's and my search for Truth and knows and appreciates our style of life better than any other single person, I think. His partnership with me in the search, in my grief and now in carrying on with the Christian origins project mean so much that it seems insignificant to mention all the things he has done to help bring this manuscript to completion.

It is my hope that the story of this search will contribute to the search for Truth.

Diane Kennedy Pike

In Our Home
Santa Barbara, California
Seven weeks after Jim's death

*SEARCH*

# A SHORT DRIVE INTO THE WILDERNESS

"Do you think we have enough room to turn around?" I asked, carefully sizing up our predicament. Jim and I had just dropped down the side of a hill and had come to a spot where the road we were on, though it appeared to go into the dry creek bed ahead and on across, was impassable. A washout between the end of the road and the bottom of the creek bed made too wide a gap for our little Ford Cortina to bridge.

"Yes," Jim said. "I'll stay here and guide you. There's no other choice but to turn around and go back."

He stood near the edge of the wadi (eroded creek bed or canyon), watching and directing as I pulled forward and then back, maneuvering the car. When I got it almost at a right angle to the road itself, I pulled as far forward as I could. Then I began backing up. "Can I go any farther?" I asked.

"Yes, keep on coming, keep on coming," Jim motioned from the left side of the car. Suddenly the right wheel dropped into a deep rut and I lost traction. Jim ran around the car as I tried to make it move forward. "There's no point in that," he cried out. "The wheel just spins." I got out and joined him.

The right rear wheel was in a rut so deep that it did not touch bottom. We put some rocks underneath it and I tried driving it out again. The wheel spun. "You're just wearing the rubber down," Jim called out, his voice strained. "We're really in trouble."

"I know," I murmured. I began to get a sick feeling in the pit of my stomach. Surely, there must be a way to get out.

It was about 2:45 in the afternoon.

At noon that day, the first of September, Jim and I had left the Intercontinental Hotel in Jerusalem to go for a short drive in our rented car. It had been our plan since before we left the United States that at some point during our stay in Israel we would hire a guide with a jeep to drive us out into the desert above the hills and caves of Qumrân—where the Dead Sea Scrolls were found—so that we could see the wilderness in which the Qumrân covenanters had spent their time meditating and fasting. That same wilderness, our research suggested, was the one Jesus went into after his baptism. The New Testament reports that he spent forty days fasting there and was tempted by the devil.

Jim and I had wanted to get a feeling for that wilderness. The map we had been given when we rented our Ford Cortina from Avis at the airport showed a road—a tertiary road to be sure, but nevertheless a road—which went into the very area we wanted to see. We were both delighted to find that we could drive there ourselves with no need of having a guide. We only wanted to get a feeling for the area—to drink it all in, as Jim said so many times. We didn't need a guide for that.

With no thought that we were doing anything out of the ordinary, we had started out of Jerusalem on the road toward Jericho. At a little store along the way we had purchased two Cokes to take along in case we got thirsty. The map we were using indicated that we could take an unpaved road off the main road fairly near Jerusalem and connect up with the one which went into the wilderness. We searched for the road, but had difficulty finding it. After several false starts, we found a dirt road which seemed to go in the right direction and started down it.

The scenery was beautiful. There were Arab villages on both sides of the road on hillsides, and a very dry riverbed off to our left, which we believed to be the valley of Kidron. We commented about the strange beauty and I took some pictures. Each time I stopped to take a picture Jim made a comment manifesting minor impatience. "I don't see what that really shows," he would say. He never liked taking pictures while traveling, but he loved sharing them with friends when we got home.

"It helps capture the mood," I responded. "It shows what the houses look like and gives you a feeling for the desert." We both sensed that feeling—an indescribable sense of elation which the clear air and expansiveness create, unlike anything I have ever experienced before.

The road had been good, but it did not take us out into the wilderness. We had been driving at the edge of villages instead. After fifteen or twenty minutes the road had dropped into and crossed a narrow valley, and at the top of the next hill we had come upon a group of Israeli soldiers.

None of the men knew English and since we spoke no Hebrew we had difficulty communicating. We showed them our map, pointing to where we thought we were. They in turn tried to show us our location on their Hebrew map, which was much more detailed and complicated. Finally they gave up trying to explain to us and merely pointed us back the way we had come and indicated we should go to the left in order to get to

Bethlehem, which, in order to simplify things, is where we had said we were going.

Following the soldiers' instructions, we came almost immediately to a paved road which took us through a small Arab village and connected up with what we knew to be the lower of two roads to Bethlehem—the older of the two. We located ourselves on our map and followed the road all the way into Bethlehem. Jim, who was watching the map, had figured out that we could go just to the other side of Bethlehem and take a road back which would connect up with the one we wanted, leading out into the desert.

We drove into Nativity Square in Bethlehem just before 1 P.M., went to a little food stand to buy two large, cold Cokes, sat in the shade to enjoy them and then went on our way. Following the signs out of Bethlehem to Herodium, we had proceeded on a paved road of the secondary type—not a main highway, but blacktopped. In a very few minutes we had come to the village of Herodium. Passing what looked like ruins on the top of the hill, I asked, "Should we stop?"

"No," Jim replied. "I don't really know what it is. We can come back another time. Let's go on."

I always did the driving and Jim watched the map—and more often than not read newspapers, magazines or books, sharing important articles and insights with me by reading out loud. This afternoon, however, he had been giving his full attention to the map, the road and the desert. "Watch for a dirt road which goes off to the left," he said at one point. "It will take us out into the wilderness."

Soon we came to a place where there was a sign in Hebrew pointing to the left on a dirt road. We didn't know what the sign meant, but it seemed to match the road on the map, so we started down it. Very shortly thereafter we came to a place where an identical sign pointed to the right up a rather steep hill, while the road we were on continued around the mountain to the left. Jim said the sign probably pointed to some historical site—a building or something—and that we wanted the main road, so we took the lower one.

Almost immediately we dropped into a very loose bed of white rock resting in dry clay dust. It was very difficult driving as the rocks shifted under the weight of the car, which then sank lower into the roadbed; it was rather like driving in mud. "Take it very slowly," Jim cautioned. "We don't want anything to happen to the car."

"I will," I promised and soon we were out again on dry, firm clay. The road was quite good, though still rocky. On our left was a canyon, a shallow wadi, and ahead of us were hills and mountains as far as we could see.

As we rounded the mountain, we had met three Arabs riding on donkeys: two men, and a woman following behind. They waved at us and we waved back and smiled. To Jim I said, "You notice the woman is riding last in the group!"

"Where else?" he asked and we both laughed. Our view was, of course, that women are entirely equal with men in their potential, and we had hoped to be able to contribute as a couple to the further realization in our culture of the beautiful freedom that can come from experiencing that parity in man-woman relationships.

Meeting the Arabs had contributed to our feeling that we were on a regularly traveled road, as had several other observations we made. As we drove along we took note of the fact that we could see animal droppings from time to time. Farther down the road we had seen a

Bedouin woman with her children going our way—though on the other side of the wadi—with a herd of goats and sheep. And we had seen road markers—three broad stripes of white, blue and white paint marked on rocks, or several rocks piled one on top of the other like those often used for trail markings—all along the way. The feeling of security these signs of life and of use of the road had given us lasted for the entire journey.

Most of the road was quite rocky and rough, though passable. Occasionally we would drop into shallow dry creek beds which were full of large rocks. We drove through them, usually with some difficulty, until we emerged on the other bank where the road continued. Jim kept urging me to go very slowly so that the rocks would not fly up and break something under the car. He didn't have to convince me of the danger: I drove very cautiously.

Once we came to a place where the road seemed literally to end. Jim jumped out of the car and ran down to the right and across the wadi, quite a deep riverbed, and called back, "It's all right. It is a road."

I felt extremely anxious. "Oh no, sweetheart," I called. "Let's don't go." As I stepped out of the car, planning to join Jim where I could see what was ahead, I suddenly got sick to my stomach. I leaned over the side of the road and called to Jim. By the time he reached me the momentary sickness passed, but I had soiled my dress, my legs and my hands.

Since there was no water available, Jim got out one of our two Coca-Cola bottles and opened it on the bumper of the car, insisting that I wash myself with it.

"No, I won't do it," I said emphatically. "We only have two with us."

His response was equally emphatic. "You certainly *will*."

So I took some of the Coke and washed. Then I insisted that we not waste the remainder but drink it, and Jim agreed. Each of us took some of it, although there was not very much; about a third of it had been lost in fizz as Jim opened it.

The experience had seem slightly amusing once we were past it, and the road did go on. A sharp switchback made it necessary to back and turn the car before proceeding, but others had done it: you could see their wheel marks. So I got back into the car and, with Jim directing me, maneuvered it into position and drove it down the hill, across the dry creek bed, and up onto the other side with no difficulty at all.

When Jim joined me, I mentioned that I was afraid of crossing places like that for fear we should have to retrace our route and not be able to make it, but the fascination of the desert drew us on. In part I'm sure we had both viewed our drive as a kind of challenge or adventure; but mainly it was the security each of us felt when we were together that had caused us not to be deterred by the rough road. Nothing seemed too difficult for us to handle or too threatening for us to face together.

Once Jim said, "I don't know why they would mark this as a road on the map!" But both of us agreed that if it *was* marked as a road, it was because it was passable. Moreover, we kept feeling that though the going had been rough, it would have been worse to turn around and go back over all that distance than to continue to the end of the road. Thus we had driven steadily on.

We had perhaps been driving about an hour when we came to a place where a road went off to the left, up and over a ridge of hills. We stopped there, studied the map and determined our location. By our best calculation it was the road to the right which we wanted. It would take us over the top of Qumrân, we thought, whereas the one to the left would go more directly back to the main road, bypassing most of the Qumrân wilderness area.

"Sweetheart," I said, "the one to the left looks like a better road."

"Yes," he answered, "but if we go to the left now, we'll miss what we came out here for, which was to see the hills—the wilderness—above Qumrân. We're not going to miss that, having come this far."

I agreed. I sensed deep inside of me that to miss that would be a great mistake.

Having turned to the right, however, we came almost immediately to a washout in the road. We backed up, crossed a wadi and started up the hill on the other road. Then Jim looked back. "There's a way to go there," he observed.

"Where?" I asked.

"On the other road," he replied. I stopped the car and turned around in my seat.

"See?" Jim said, pointing to tracks which had been made by jeeps driving up from the creek bed onto the other road, beyond the washout.

I was reluctant to go at first, but Jim said, "It looks easy compared to other things we've done." I had to agree, so we backed up into the creek bed and drove down it to the place where we could return to the road.

Having made that turn, we were sure we were very close to Qumrân; the juncture we had located on our map indicated that.

Once or twice I said rather nervously, "Sweetheart, it looks like endless desert, just endless desert."

## A SHORT DRIVE INTO THE WILDERNESS

But Jim replied, "It can't be endless desert. The map doesn't show endless desert."

I could see nothing but mountains, so I tried again: "Darling, look. Just endless desert. Endless."

Jim's logic dominated. "It can't be endless desert. The map doesn't show endless desert."

Though I had a growing sense of uneasiness, and I suspect Jim felt it too, basically I agreed with him that it couldn't be endless desert. And more important, I *wanted* to go on. I was enjoying the desert beauty and my uneasiness about the road was tempered by the fact that it was difficult only in spots.

Farther on, while trying to cross a dry creek bed, we got our car stuck in the rocks. We feared we were in trouble then, but as we began to try to dig the car out, two Bedouin appeared off to the right. We waved them over.

When the Bedouin reached us, we asked them if they would help us move our car. Though they spoke no English, they could see what our difficulty was and immediately got into position to help Jim push while I drove. With not too much effort, the car lurched forward and onto the road again. We thanked the Bedouin, who were both very young, and Jim tried to offer them money, but they refused it.

Then Jim pointed down the road and said, "Is the Dead Sea that way?" They obviously understood nothing. "Qumrân?" he queried, hoping they would recognize the name. They registered no response. He tried to ask them if it was all right for us to go that way and they made a series of motions with their hands and arms, pointing and gesturing as if to indicate a sudden drop, or a cliff. We were not sure what they meant, but we did know that at the top of the hills in back of Qumrân there were steep cliffs falling in an eastward direction to the Dead Sea. So we thought they must be indicating we were near our goal. Again we thanked them and started the car. The Bedouin turned back to their herds, apparently unconcerned.

We had driven quite a long distance on a rather good road. The scenery was fantastic. Off to our left were deep wadis and in the distance on all sides were incredibly beautiful parched hills—bleached almost white by the sun. Barren, dry. A strange kind of beauty—different from any I had ever known. We had been caught up in it and in the hushed sense of awe which its desolate loveliness inspired.

But now we really were stuck. Without saying anything, I went around to the right rear wheel and began to dig. "What are you doing?" Jim asked.

"There has to be a way," I replied.

I dug as deep as I could under the wheel. Then I filled the hole with rocks and tried to knock the rut in front of the right rear wheel down so that the car could move straight forward. Jim stood and watched.

"Let's try again," I said. I got in and started the motor. Jim lifted the car from behind and tried to push it. The right wheel spun.

"It's no use," he said.

We both worked, alternating efforts, trying to get a firm bed of rocks under the wheel. Each time we would try again, our nervousness would grow. Jim was lifting and pushing while I sat in the driver's seat.

Finally Jim said, "I'm feeling faint."

"Oh, darling, please sit in the shade," I implored, concerned now about Jim too. There was a small shaded area next to the nearby rocks, and a very slight movement of air around the rocks felt almost like a breeze. I had found it earlier as I rested while Jim was working.

"*You're* in the sun," Jim protested.

"I'm OK for now. You rest and then we'll trade again." Jim sat in the shade till I could work no more. I stumbled over toward him.

"Here, dear," he said, his voice manifesting deep concern. "Sit down."

I leaned against the rock. "No," I said, "I think I'll just rest here a minute." Jim went back to the car and began working with the rocks.

Soon he said, "Let's try once more." But the results were the same: the spinning, slipping sound signaled futility. Jim went back to the shade and I lay down on my side by the wheel to study the situation. Suddenly I noticed that the frame of the car was caught on the high, back ridge of the rut.

I went to the ignition, got the key, opened the trunk and took out the jack. "If we could jack the car up," I said, "perhaps we could get it up high enough to push it forward off the jack and out of the rut." Jim joined me. I explained about the frame being caught on the rut and he agreed the jack might help.

"Where can we put the jack?" Jim asked.

"We'll find a place," I said confidently.

But we couldn't figure out how to make the jack work. I looked for directions for assembling the jack. There were none. I searched the glove compartment for a driver's manual. There was none. My heart sank.

"The base of the jack is missing," Jim said.

"It can't be," I said, not wanting to believe it. "Let's take it over there and study it. I'm sure we can figure out how to make it work." We both sat down in the shade of the rock and for a long time I studied the construction of the jack to see how it worked. I had always scored high on mechanical understanding and I was sure I could figure it out. But by the action of the pump on this jack and the way it moved, it seemed apparent that whatever it was supposed to sit on simply was not there. If you turned it upside down, then the pumping action wouldn't work as there was no tension on it.

Jim looked at it and said simply, "The base just isn't there." He also had the ability to figure out mechanical devices in practically no time at all, but neither of us could see how this could function without a base.

We both went back to the trunk of the car to find the missing part. We searched the entire trunk to no avail. Jim asked me to check behind the spare tire. There was nothing. "Sometimes the base of the jack is used to hold the spare tire in place," I commented, but the piece of metal which held the spare was hinged to the floor of the trunk.

Weeks later I discovered there was nothing wrong with the jack. It was a European one-piece tool which we had never seen before and didn't know how to operate. But I did not know it in the desert and, in my desperation, I took the small crowbar which was part of the equipment and began using it as a chisel on the rock which was hanging up the right rear side of the car. Jim went and sat down in the shade by the rock and I lay down with my head in the shade of the car, chipping away at the dry clay rock.

"Come and rest," Jim called.

"I'm OK," I insisted. "Let me work a little more."

When I felt I had made some progress, I got back in the car and put the key back in to try to start it. Jim got in place to lift and push. But I couldn't get the ignition key out of the lock position.

For the first time I began to really panic. I couldn't

get the key to move at all. I moved the gearshift back and forth but nothing helped. "What's wrong?" Jim asked. He sat down in the back seat on the right side where there was some shade, but suffocatingly hot air.

"I can't get the key to turn," I said, nearly frantic.

"What does that mean?" Jim asked.

"I don't know," I said.

"Here," Jim said, coming to my side of the car. "Let me try." I got out. Jim sat down and tried, but he couldn't get it to turn either.

I was wandering in circles in the hot sun when suddenly I realized I was losing control. I said out loud to myself, meaning it partly for Jim, but mainly for myself, "We can't panic. We must keep our heads about us. It's important that we think and that we do things logically." Gradually I calmed myself down and tried to remember everything my father ever taught me about cars.

A memory flashed through my mind and I got an idea. "Let me try it again," I said quickly. Jim got out and I jumped up and down on the running board, trying to jar the car, before I sat down. Then I moved the wheel around to a different position, and somehow in the process the lock released and I was able to turn the ignition on again. We both heaved tremendous sighs of relief.

Jim got behind the car and tried to lift and push as I started the motor. The wheel spun.

I got out again and my mind raced for another idea. "We need clothes or something to help it get traction," I said. Jim looked puzzled. Then I thought of the rubber floor mats. I pulled two out and tried putting them under the wheel. I got back in the car and started the motor. Jim watched as the rubber mats spun all the way through and out the back.

"Wait a minute," he called. I sat in the driver's seat. He

tried replacing them several times, using rocks above and below, adding two more from the back seat, doubling them up. Each time they spun through.

Finally Jim said, "Now try." I started the motor. "God!" he cried out. I stopped at once. Then to me: "I almost lost my arm! I tried to hold onto the mat and the wheel tore it out of my hands, almost taking me along."

"Oh, darling," I sighed. "I'm sorry." I knew it was futile. Nothing seemed to help. The car was simply impossible to move. After all the work—the pushing, the lifting, the chipping and the digging—there seemed to be no way whatsoever we could get it out of the rut. We put it into neutral and tried together to lift and push the car, but with no results.

By this time it was nearly four o'clock—more than an hour since the car got stuck. We were very hot and very tired. Our heads felt dizzy from the heat of the sun and we felt weak from the tremendous expenditure of energy. A decision had to be made.

"What do you think we should do?" Jim asked. "Should we sit here by this rock in the shade until it gets dark?"

It seemed to hit both of us at once: "I was just thinking of what the guide told us at the top of Masada[1] last year —about only being able to survive in the desert for seven hours without water," I observed slowly.

"I was thinking of the very same thing," Jim said, looking worried.

"It's a long way back the way we came. A terribly long

[1] A desert fortress, built by Herod, which was the last hold-out of the Zealot fighters in the Jewish Revolt of 66 A.D. Ten thousand Roman soldiers fought against 960 Zealots for three years after the Fall of Jerusalem before finally defeating them in 73 A.D. The site is being restored by archaeologists and is open to tourists. Bishop Pike and the author had visited there together in May of 1968.

way. It seems that if time is of the essence, it would be better to start walking toward the Dead Sea where we know there is water at Qumrân."

Jim nodded assent, "Professor Flusser will just have to understand," he said sadly.

## IF I DIE HERE

We had a dinner engagement scheduled for 7:30 P.M. that Monday evening with Professor David Flusser of Hebrew University—a noted New Testament scholar and practicing Jew with whom Jim had worked rather closely for several years—and his wife. We could both see we would probably miss the appointment, and Jim's remark revealed his characteristic concern for the other person. He would not have offended Professor Flusser for anything: he would just have to understand.

"Take your wallet and passport," Jim said, getting up from his resting position against the rock. He reached in the car to get his trousers, which he had taken off because of the tremendous heat, our map, and the remaining Coca-Cola. I grabbed my camera and what I thought was my wallet.

"Shall I leave the keys in the car?" I asked.

"No, take them along," Jim replied. I tucked them down in my bra.

"How will we open the Coke?" Jim puzzled. I couldn't think of a way. "How did I do it before?" he asked.

"On the bumper of the car," I said.

"Maybe we should open it here," Jim responded. "I'll try not to lose as much of it as we would if we had to break it." It was so hot, however, that nearly a third of it was lost in fizz despite all efforts on Jim's part to prevent it.

17

Each of us took a little sip—we were so thirsty—and then started on our way, Jim carrying the remainder of the Coke.

We left the car entirely open, the trunk lid up, the tools lying around, all the doors open, the rubber mats around the rear wheel—just as it was when we were working with it.

As we set out walking in the dry creek bed, toward the Dead Sea, we made a couple of quick decisions. We would stay in the wadi in order not to lose our sense of direction, feeling sure the canyon would lead directly to the Dead Sea and knowing that the road did not, and we would talk as little as possible. We were already aware that every word dried out our mouths terribly, and we knew we should conserve all of our energy, keeping our mouths closed as we walked so the air would not dry them unnecessarily. When possible we would walk in the shade, but we felt we should keep going because each passing hour would make our survival more problematic.

As we started, Jim was carrying his trousers—because it was so hot—and was hiking in his loafers, undershorts and T-shirt. His green and yellow sport shirt covered his head. I had on a light cotton dress, which buttoned down the front, and thong sandals. I unbuttoned my dress part way to making walking easier, and used the map to shade my head. Both of us were perspiring heavily.

"This reminds me of the movie *Lawrence of Arabia*," I commented.

"What?" Jim sounded puzzled.

"Did you ever see it?"

"Yes," he replied.

"Well, I was thinking of those incredible desert scenes with the blinding sun beating on the sand. I remember how thirsty I was at intermission." The comment was almost small talk, but it reflected my growing realization that, though there was no sand in this desert, the sun was beating down on our heads and backs and dehydrating our bodies. And we had just begun to walk.

Each time I stepped on a rock in my thong sandals my foot turned; it was very difficult going for me. Jim got quite a ways ahead of me, walking with his determined, steady pace. Feeling rather nervous, I said, "Sweetheart, I'd really prefer if we walked together." But he walked right on, seeming almost not to hear. I thought, "It's probably better that he go on if he is able to. That will encourage me to keep moving in order to stay with him." We went on in silence.

After a half hour or so, Jim paused and said, "I'm going to put my T-shirt on my head like I did at Masada. The air passing through it should be cooling since it is soaked with sweat," he explained.

"Good," I said. He handed me his other shirt and I put it on my head loosely so that the air would catch in it, creating a slight breeze down my back. I folded the map and held it under my arm. To free my hands I started to tuck my wallet into my bra. "Oh, sweetheart," I gasped, "I brought my cosmetics case instead of my wallet!"

Jim paused momentarily. Then he said, "We can't go back now." Of course, I knew he was right, but I felt so stupid for having made such a mistake. It seemed important under these circumstances that we make no mistakes.

While we were stopped, rearranging our head coverings and readjusting the things we were carrying, Jim suggested we finish the Coke. "Maybe we should save it,"

I said tentatively, feeling terribly thirsty but wanting to use good judgment.

"I have to have some now," Jim said, "or I can't go on." I knew how thirsty and tired we both were, so I agreed. We shared the remainder of the Coke and left the bottle in the wadi.

From time to time, though very rarely, we came to some shade which we could walk in by the side of a cliff, finding tremendous relief just by getting the direct heat off our heads. The sun had a dizzying effect. Once Jim commented he felt as if he were drunk. "It's been years since I've had that feeling," he said. Jim was a recovered alcoholic, having been completely dry for over five years.

"We *must* be going east toward the Dead Sea," I said reassuringly at one point, "because the sun is behind us." But later Jim observed that he thought we were going south. "That's impossible," I responded. "We couldn't be going south. If anything, according to the map, we would be going north."

It didn't dawn on either of us that we were in a winding canyon, though that should have seemed perfectly obvious, and as it turned out Jim was right about our direction—we were headed southeast. We were both still confident we were in Wadi Qumrân, however, and that we couldn't possibly be more than two miles from the Dead Sea.

While the creek bed was still relatively level and quite wide, I observed, "We could have driven here, couldn't we?" Jim nodded affirmatively. A wave of remorse swept over me that instead of trying to get our car down in the wadi we had tried to turn around. "We might have made it," I thought. Second thoughts only torture—they don't guarantee what might have been.

At several points along the way I stopped to take pictures of Jim walking ahead of me and of the surrounding territory. Once Jim said, "Don't stop to take pictures now," his voice indicating he felt it was a waste of both time and energy—and perhaps even inappropriate.

"We'll want to have pictures of this once we get out," I explained. "People wouldn't believe the kind of terrain we are in."

Later I commented, "Sweetheart, I'm scared."

"So am I," was his only reply.

After a pause, "Well, I guess we've learned a few lessons," I observed, thinking primarily of our not having brought any water along.

"We'll talk about that after we get out of here," Jim answered flatly.

It occurred to me once that if Jim should faint I wouldn't know what to do. I kept urging him to get into the shade whenever he could—an unnecessary exercise since he was eager to do just that.

After we'd been walking for what seemed like a long time, I realized my mouth was getting extremely dry, so I tried very hard to work up some saliva in it. When I had enough to wet the inside of my own mouth and still have a little extra, I turned and waited for Jim, who by this time had fallen somewhat behind me.

"Are you able to get any saliva at all in your mouth?" I asked. He shook his head, his eyes revealing the depth of his concern for us both.

"Here. Take some of mine," I offered, stepping close to him. "Don't swallow. Just roll it around on the inside of your mouth and try to get as much of your own saliva flowing as you can."

I put my mouth on his and passed to him what seemed a pathetically small amount of moisture. He received it without comment and we began walking again.

Once we were into the second hour of walking, a nervous feeling that we were not playing any more, that this was not a joke, that we could really be in trouble, began to settle over me. But I had no way even to imagine the extent or nature of the problems ahead. Neither of us knew enough about the desert to suspect or fear that. It still seemed to me that we would soon be coming upon Qumrân, that we would be able to make it, that it was possible to get out.

But not all our thoughts were bleak. Once Jim remarked lightly, "Maybe we'll stumble upon a Dead Sea Scroll in one of these caves." I smiled, actually thinking how great that would be. And it didn't seem impossible.

Another time he said, "No matter what, I don't regret coming here. It is beautiful."

"I don't either," was my response.

And we both meant that. It *was* beautiful—the land was magnificent and powerful, overwhelming in its beauty as well as its climate.

At length we saw ahead of us some iron rods sticking up. "Could that be water?" Jim asked.

At first I didn't understand what he meant. Then, bringing the rods into focus and realizing they could be water pipes—even faucets, I responded, "Perhaps."

Hope surging, we picked up our speed a little. As we got nearer we could see they were only old pieces of pipe which had been used to hold some kind of fence. Our spirits fell. I felt a fantastic drain of energy in Jim. His disappointment was so great I felt I needed to muster hope for us both.

Just to the right of those pipes, the wadi began to get deeper, dropping into what looked like a kind of canyon. "Now we're getting closer," I said, trying to spark his hope again. "We should stay on the left side, toward the top." I was trying to speak with assurance. "I remember very clearly that at Qumrân when we climbed up into the caves, the deepest part of the wadi was way down below us."

"Was it?" Jim asked, obviously not remembering—nor making an effort.

I went right on. "And remember when we were climbing down from the caves and you and Scott tried to get down into the center of the canyon? You got stuck, remember? And Scott was helping you down when I took a picture of you. Remember?"

Jim registered no response.

I remembered vividly: My brother Scott, who, together with Jim's daughter Connie, was traveling with us, had climbed to the top of the mountains—incredibly far up—to a cave which he had spotted. Even Jim and I had climbed awfully high. I also remembered how deep the canyon was below.

Since Jim made no response, I said, "We'll walk up here," pointing to a level that was quite near the top of the canyon. There was a sloping ledge to walk on. Though Jim apparently had no recollection of the Qumrân canyon, he followed me, knowing my ability to recall details of places and locations was far greater than his, though his memory excelled mine in almost every other regard.

So it was that we started walking on the upper level of the canyon. It got rougher and steeper the farther we walked, and the rocks grew sharper. The going was more and more difficult and we were soon climbing at rather steep angles to the cliffs, making it easy to turn an ankle, to stumble or to trip on rocks jutting up.

We were both feeling very exhausted. We had by now been walking for over an hour.

Jim said, "I'm going to have to rest."

Consciously subordinating my feelings, which matched Jim's, to my thoughts, I responded, "I think we should keep going, sweetheart."

After several more minutes of climbing, Jim said, "I really *have* to rest." I spotted an overhanging rock nearby which formed a shallow cave.

"Okay," I said. "Here's a little cave. Let's rest here."

We both collapsed on our backs, our heads inside the cave. Our bodies were almost entirely shaded by the rock. Only our feet remained in the sun. Jim was to my left on the flatter side of the cave. I was lying on a slight slope which made resting uncomfortable, though changing positions seemed almost impossible I was so exhausted. Jim used his suit pants as a pillow to lay his head on, and I used his shirt which I had had over my head. We were lying on rocks, but to clear them away would have taken more energy than we had.

"Is urine poisonous?" Jim asked.

"I don't know," was my response. "Why?"

"Well, I could urinate," he explained. "I hate to waste the water if we could use it."

I don't think I answered. To waste water seemed unthinkable, yet I hesitated to say I thought we should use urine to drink. We lay in silence, except for the sound of Jim's heart, which was beating hard and fast. I said nothing, but listened intently till it began to slow down. Though his heart had always been in perfect condition, I was afraid the strain might somehow affect it.

We had no more than stretched out in the cave when flies descended on us in swarms. Every inch of exposed skin was completely covered with them. We were so exhausted and dehydrated—though our skin was sweaty—that we couldn't even shoo the flies off. I remember resenting them. "What do you live on when I'm not here?"

I wondered. "How dare you use the moisture from my skin for your survival when I need it so desperately!"

Suddenly Jim put his hand on my lips and I felt the cooling touch of water. I realized that he had urinated just a little bit on his hand and was giving me the first moisture. I licked it off and swallowed it, grateful for anything wet. Then I heard Jim wash some around in his mouth and spit it out. When he gave me more, I drank it —drank it because it was wet. The taste seemed irrelevant. He took more in his mouth and again spit it out.

Then he let his urine flow and we both took it and washed it all over our faces and arms. It was unbelievably refreshing. And even though immediately afterward the flies covered our bodies again, the feeling of relief from the intense dehydration persisted for some time.

It was after five in the afternoon when we collapsed in the cave. The sun was low enough in the sky that I could tell we didn't have much daylight left for travel. For that reason, after I could tell Jim's heart had stopped pounding, I sat up.

"Sweetheart," I began, "has your heart slowed down?"

"Um hmm," he responded.

"I really think we have to go on before it gets dark."

"All right," Jim said, rolling over on his side and beginning to raise himself up.

It was hard for both of us to start out, but I seemed to have a little more energy, strength and drive left than Jim did. He followed close behind me as we began to climb on the cliffs again. The going was very difficult and I was aware of how little strength either of us had.

Suddenly I looked up and saw what I thought was the back of the caves at Qumrân. At the top of a cliff there was a rectangular cave opening which looked just like one Jim and I had climbed to the year before. We had later learned it was a water aqueduct and not a natural cave.

I was very encouraged. "Sweetheart, that's Qumrân!" I said with great hope. "It really is; it's Qumrân."

"Where?" Jim asked.

"Remember that aqueduct we crawled through?" Jim nodded affirmatively. "Yes, I remember."

"That's it," I said pointing. "Let's keep going," I urged. "We're almost there."

So we pressed on, but as we rounded the next bend in the canyon, it became apparent that it wasn't Qumrân at all. The other side of the canyon didn't look anything like it and beyond, as far as we could see, were more mountains and more canyons.

My heart sank. Jim said, "I just can't go on. I have to sleep. I can't go any farther. My legs feel like a hiker's on the day after a hike."

"Oh, please, sweetheart," I pleaded. "We need to go on."

"I just can't," he said in a sadly faltering tone. "I have to sleep."

I felt I had already pressed him beyond his strength on a false hope, and I too was exhausted. So I agreed to rest. There was a flat rock just above where we were walking, so we flopped down on it. This time Jim was on my right. Again our heads were to the back of the rock, but now there was no shade. The sun was very low, however—shortly it would go down behind the mountains. So we simply collapsed on the rock in the sun.

Jim said he was going to try to sleep.

"All right," I said quietly.

He tucked his trousers under his head like a pillow. I lay very still, aware we were again literally covered with flies—I felt them crawling all over me and was amazed at how little they bothered. It was almost as though my senses were numbed by the exhaustion.

"Now I understand why the Bedouin wear the clothes they do," I commented. Jim murmured recognition of my remark, but said nothing. I wasn't sure he knew what I meant, but I didn't have the strength to explain that I saw two reasons for clothes which covered the entire body: to keep the flies off and to keep the body moisture in.

Jim flopped his left arm over on me. I knew it was a sign of affection and of his wanting to stay in touch even as he slept. We always slept close together. But it exhausted me to have his arm rest on me. It was as though the weight would crush me. I said, "I'm sorry, sweetheart," and pushed his arm down beside me. His hand touched me slightly on my side and I said, "That's fine." I had never before felt that touching drained energy. To the contrary. But I just couldn't stand it there in the desert. What a dreadful, sad feeling it was to be that exhausted.

After what seemed like a long time had passed, I began to feel restless. I couldn't sleep, so I sat up. The sun was almost down to the ridge of the canyon. It was late and would soon be dark. I was sitting with my arms around my knees, not really thinking about what we should do but concerned about time passing.

Jim said, "If you're going to be sitting up like that, would you please fan the flies off my face?" Without saying anything, I moved around to the right side of his head and sat on a slight slope. It was difficult to maintain my balance there, but I took the map and tried to slowly fan his face in order to keep the flies away.

It took so much strength, so *much* strength, to fan the flies, that after only three or four motions I said, "I'm sorry, I just can't." I was amazed at my inability to comply with such a small request.

I fell down beside him and lay there, resting, for several minutes. Finally I said, "Are you sure you're not going to be able to go on?"

"Yes," Jim replied. "I can't go on. I've got to sleep."

"Well," I said slowly, "maybe I should go for help."

"I think you should," Jim responded. "Tell them to bring lots of water. Tell them I'm feeling faint—to bring something for that. Tell them even to bring whisky; I'd even try whisky."

I was moved to tears by that. Such a big concession revealed the degree of his distress. I smiled and said tenderly, "Of course you would, sweetheart."

It was beginning to get dark as I started off to the left, planning to climb out of the canyon for help. I didn't think it through. I didn't know where I was going or how I would get help. I just started.

But when I tried to lift my body up over the sheer rocks to the left of where Jim was lying, I simply did not have the energy, the strength in my arms, to lift my body. I got a terrible, sick feeling in my stomach: What if I were to get up there and then collapse somewhere. There I would be by myself—and Jim would be down below.

So I climbed back down to the rock where Jim was and collapsed beside him, on my back, with my head by his feet. My head hit his right foot as I fell. "I'm sorry," I said weakly.

"No, it's all right," Jim answered. My head was touching his foot as I lay beside him. I was glad to be in contact with him, even if it was only through his shoe.

"It's impossible to climb out, darling. It's sheer rock straight up. It's *impossible* to climb out," I explained, my energy depleted.

"Why did we ever leave the bottom of the canyon?" Jim asked desperately.

"I don't know," I answered. I had forgotten momentarily and it was too much strain to try to remember. Besides, now it seemed a wrong decision, and I had made it. Now it seemed impossible to get out. Neither of us saw the contradiction in logic; obviously it would have been even more difficult had we stayed at the bottom of the canyon.

I said, "Sweetheart, if we're going to die in the desert, I want to die here beside you." For the first time death seemed the most likely possibility.

"OK," was his only reply. We lay for a long time in the silence. Then I had a sudden flash of memory of several lengthy conversations Jim and I had had just a few weeks before about our inability to comprehend why a person with any degree of rational control in a crisis situation would not do everything possible to save the life of another.

"Diane," I thought. "If you were to stay here to die beside Jim it would be purely selfish. It would be only because you wanted to be with him, to be beside him when you die. If you get up and go, there is a possibility, a slight possibility, that you might be able to get help. You have to go on."

I also had another brief flash, a momentary one but an important one, I think. If I were to stay there and we were both to die on that rock in the desert and someone were to find us sometime in the future, they might think it was suicide. And they would have been so wrong, so wrong. Whereas if I started out for help and died somewhere along the way, at least they would know that we had been trying to get help.

When the decision to go was made, there fell over me a

great sense of calm and peace. All fear was gone—all anxiety relieved. No more fluttering of the stomach. No more nervousness. I had no fear of dying—and no fear of going off by myself. I had to go in order not to distort the meaning of the life Jim and I had shared together.

"Sweetheart, I'm going to go for help." I sensed either decision was all right with him.

"OK," Jim said. "Tell them to bring lots of water."

"If I die in the desert, you'll know that I went because I love you and I was trying to get help for you," I said.

"I know that," Jim responded. "I love you too, and if I die here"—his voice broke slightly—"I am at peace, and I have no regrets."

I knew what that last statement meant in the over-all context of our relationship because we had used it over and over again. Both of us felt it very deeply about all of the events which made up our lives. We often said, when we started to regret something, "No, no. I don't regret anything. Not anything. Because had the slightest little detail been different we might not have met one another." So we would not have changed anything in our pasts—not even the difficult and painful things. Jim was reaffirming that feeling, bringing it into the present.

I was deeply moved and knew he shared my sense of calm. He did not fear death either. We were both at peace about that.

"Sweetheart, I'm going to the very bottom of the canyon," I explained. "I'll climb down all the way, and I'll go at the bottom of the canyon all the way to the Dead Sea." I felt that was the only certain way of reaching the Dead Sea. I couldn't possibly get lost there, I reasoned.

Jim responded, "Perhaps after I've slept awhile I can follow."

"All right," I replied as I got up to go. I didn't say good-bye. I didn't feel it was good-bye. I knew I was leaving him and I felt that we would probably both die in the desert, but it was not good-bye.

"Leave everything with me so your hands are free for climbing," Jim urged.

"OK," I agreed. I took my cosmetics case out of my bra and left it with Jim. My sunglasses, the map, my camera and his sport shirt were already lying on the rock by his head.

As I left, I saw Jim turn over on his left side to get into a better position for sleep. I had gone only a short way when I heard him cry out, "Diane!"

It frightened me. "What is it?" I called back.

"Tell them to bring lots of water—and yell 'help me' all the way along."

"Oh, my God," I said, catching my breath. "I thought you had fallen. Yes, of course I'll yell 'help me.' Of course I'll tell them to bring water."

I looked at my watch. It was 6:10 P.M. There had been something almost frantic about Jim's crying out like that and about the echo of his cry against the canyon wall. It jarred me—resounding with a kind of emptiness. That was the last time I heard his voice.

## THE WEB OF LIFE

I climbed all the way down to the bottom of the canyon, dropped myself to its floor and began to make my way along. At the bottom of the wadi the rocks were completely different from those on the cliff wall above. Most of them were very large, smooth boulders which appeared to have been rounded off by rushing water. I had a feeling that great rapids and waterfalls would be created there during rainy seasons. The canyon was deep and narrow, forcing a constriction of passing water. Considering the extremely solid, dry clay which made up the rest of the terrain, it was easy to visualize the flash desert floods I had heard about.

I climbed along, working my way among the boulders as best I could. Eventually I began coming upon small trees growing on the rocks. They seemed to be evergreen trees of some kind and I rejoiced at the sign of life. "There must be water nearby," I thought.

The faint light of dusk remained, enabling me to see something of my immediate surroundings. I searched near the roots of the trees to see where they were getting water to sustain their life. The roots were largely exposed and looked white against the rock. But there was no water. The trees appeared to grow out of the rock itself. I didn't understand how that was possible, but my lack of comprehension only made me feel more of a stranger to the desert.

Before long the bottom of the canyon began to deepen rapidly. I found myself dropping from one level to another in order to continue, occasionally hanging with my arms fully extended and still not touching the next level. Finally I came to a place where it looked as though I would have to drop over ten feet if I was to continue my chosen course.

I hesitated to drop myself down, not because I was afraid, but because I knew that if I was to get help, I mustn't break a leg—and that seemed a real possibility. So I decided it was better to get out of the base of the canyon. I had to retrace my steps for quite a long way, lifting myself up, over and between the same boulders. Finally I got to the left side of the canyon again.

It never occurred to me that I would cause Jim any difficulty by changing the course I had indicated to him. I just assumed I would get back with help before he moved on. Once out of the base of the canyon, I climbed up the wall, which seemed all I could do. Eventually I got to a place where there were some ledges to walk on. They were very narrow—many of them wide enough for only one foot—but I could move forward, toward the Dead Sea.

As it grew darker, I had difficulty discerning anything more than the rocks immediately in front of me and the silhouette of the mountains against the sky. There seemed to be endless ranges of mountains in the distance, so I tried to concentrate on what was immediately before me. I watched the contour of the rock only so I could be relatively certain that there was enough of a ledge ahead on which to continue to climb. I don't remember trying to look back down into the bottom of the canyon again, or back the way I had come. I was bent on making progress toward civilization.

Time has blurred for me and the experiences I had while climbing on the walls of the canyon seem almost like one: I have no recollection of the sequence of events or the passage of time in relation to them. Yet the experiences themselves remain vividly imprinted on my memory.

Not long after I climbed out of the base of the canyon, I began to feel utterly exhausted and depleted of all energy. I had not rested since leaving Jim, and I began to realize that getting help was not going to be a simple matter of climbing for an hour or two. The mountains went on and on, still looking like endless desert and canyon. I felt my body was too exhausted to make it.

Then a strange thing began to happen. I became aware that I was communicating with my body as if it were a friend along for the trip. I didn't talk out loud to myself, but with my mind I spoke to my whole body and to the individual parts of it. As I lay on the side of the cliffs, resting against the pointed, jagged rock, I would say to my body, "Thank you for not hurting when you lie on the rocks. Thank you for resting."

Then I began to say, "We must walk all night." I knew when the sun came up neither Jim nor I would have much chance for survival, but I thought if I kept walking all night at least I would be that much closer to someone's discovering me in the morning.

So I began to say to my body, "We must walk all night long. We will walk a few minutes at a time and then rest. Get up now. Go just a little way farther, just five minutes. Then I'll let you rest again."

When I spoke lovingly to my body, it was somehow able to respond. Strength came from somewhere, and it would get up and begin to climb again. To my right hand, these words: "You must find a rock to take ahold of, a

## SEARCH

rock that will support you." It would search, looking for a rock, and finally find one to hold onto. To my right foot, these: "You must find a rock to stand on." It would probe and search until it found something that wouldn't slide or give way. Then I would speak to my left hand and my left foot in the same manner.

My body somehow made its way along, hanging on the cliffs, climbing over the rocks, going around points of jagged rocks that stuck out where there was really nothing to hang onto, climbing up sheer rock faces where there was nothing to do but to lift myself from one level to the next. I would say to the muscles in my arms, "You'll have to lift the whole body, you'll have to lift the body up." And the muscles would cooperate by lifting me.

I developed a strange kind of affection and love for this friend, my body, that was with me on this journey. I could tell the tremendous effort it was making—trying so hard to cooperate, trying to do what I was asking it to do.

As I climbed along the canyon wall I was able to keep going only a few minutes at a time. Then I just had to find a place wide enough to stretch out, laying my head and back on rocks, letting my feet dangle if need be. I had to rest. There were no flies now, since the sun was down. Only the silence surrounded me.

Each time I felt as though I would never be able to get up again. But I knew it was important to keep moving, so I would say to my body, "We will go just a little farther. Just five minutes more, and then you can rest again. We must walk all night. We must walk all night." And somehow my body would get up again and in the same loving fashion would cooperate in order to move me along.

It felt so good to rest my body that even though I was

lying on sharp rocks which dug into my skin, I felt a fantastic sense of relief. I soon began to feel an overwhelming sense of gratitude to the rocks for being there to hold my body when I needed to rest. I felt no pain when the rocks protruded into my skin—I felt gratitude and relief for any place to lie down at all.

Gradually, over the course of the journey, I developed a warm feeling of love for the rocks. I realized I wouldn't be able to travel if it weren't for the rocks. Some held firm while my hands caught hold of them, supporting my weight when I had to cling to and hang from the rocks above. Others held my feet as I felt my way along. Still others were big enough or firm enough to allow my whole body a place to recline and rest.

Not all the rocks held firm. Many broke off or came loose and fell down into the canyon, carrying others with them. But it was all right. It was as though each rock played its proper role, and I loved them all, being especially grateful to those that held me.

A special sense of identification between the rocks and my body began to develop. I was aware they were somehow of the same order of things—material manifestations of the Life Force, instruments through which and with which that Life Force worked. My body had no more "right" to life than the rocks. Each played its own part in the total pattern of things, enabling the Life Force to carry on its orderly process of birth, death and rebirth. And that was as it should be.

Far into my trek I remember catching hold of a thornbush for the first time. I realized what it was but didn't dare let go as my instinct would ordinarily have dictated, because it seemed able to support my weight. I held on and was grateful for its being there. "Thank you for holding me," I said silently to the bush.

Once I came to a thornbush big enough to lie down on. It had so much elasticity in contrast to the rocks that it felt like a feather cushion to me. The thorns were irrelevant; it was the springiness of the bush itself that supported my body and gave it rest. Whether rocks or thorns, the fact that they punctured or pressed into my body was not important. It was the rest they gave me, and the support, for which I was grateful. And it was their part in the whole order of things that made me identify with them and come to love them.

I was also grateful to my body for not causing me any pain. I could feel my flesh being torn: my legs got bumped and scraped, my feet bruised and cut, my bottom gouged, my hands and arms punctured and lacerated —but I did not suffer from the wounds. "Thank you for not hurting," I said over and over again to my body. "Thank you."

Once in stepping I turned my left ankle and sprained it badly. Out loud I said—as though speaking out loud would make a greater impact—"I know I've sprained you, but you cannot get stiff and you cannot swell up because we must walk all night." The ankle did not swell or get stiff; I was aware it had been injured, but I felt no pain.

"Thank you for not swelling," I repeated to the ankle each time I turned it again.

During certain parts of the climb on the wall of the cliff the terrain was so treacherous that I was hanging from rocks above, unable to find more than an occasional place to put a foot. Inching my way along, I tried putting my weight on my right foot at one point when there was nothing to step on. I plunged head over heels through the air toward the bottom of the canyon.

I was aware that I was falling, but I felt no fear whatsoever. "I will be killed when I hit bottom," I thought. There flashed through my mind a scene from a movie I had once seen about some climbers who tried to scale Mt. Everest. In the film, one of the members of the climbing team slipped and fell through the air to his death. If I remember correctly, he was attached to a rope. But an image of him flashed through my mind and I thought to myself, "I'm falling just like that man on Mt. Everest."

Then I struck my right elbow on a rock, breaking the fall. I reached out and back with my hands, clutching at the rocks, until I was able finally to stop myself.

I knew my elbow had been deeply cut, though I felt no pain. "The blood," I thought. "I could drink the blood." I reached over to my elbow with my left hand and tried to gather some of the blood on my fingers. The coagulation took place so quickly, however, that I was able to salvage very little of the liquid.

I was not shaken by the experience. In fact, a feeling of near elation filled me as I realized that fear of death held no power over me. I felt utterly confident that if my body died, I would go on living. The same assurance filled me with regard to Jim. This struggle was for the life of our physical bodies, but our personhood was not at stake: we would live on.

I became keenly aware that the life which flowed through my body was in continuity with the Great Life. Though that Life Force was manifest in this physical form now, it was not dependent on that material expression. Death of the body did not threaten the Great Life, and therefore it did not threaten me.

I climbed back up to where I had been climbing, as best I could determine it, and proceeded on my way.

Once when I was resting it occurred to me that there might be snakes in the desert. A great sense of joy began to arise in me. I had never had such a feeling, such a thought, before: "Oh, I hope so," my mind raced. "If there's a snake and it comes near me, I'll grab it at the base of its head and smash its head on a rock. Then I'll tear it open and eat it. There must be liquids in it." My thoughts raced on. "What if it's a poisonous snake? It doesn't matter. There will be fluids in it nevertheless and I will drink them even if they are poisonous."

Suddenly I understood people of other cultures who eat snake meat and grasshoppers. I thought, "Oh, if only there were grasshoppers, I could eat grasshoppers! They must have juice in them." And I really would have eaten them. I felt so dehydrated and drained of all energy that I would have taken any available fluid into my body, regardless of the source.

A little later I had another flash: "I wonder if there are any rabbits in the canyon? Or desert rats?" I don't recall ever thinking of killing an animal before, but if I could have caught a rabbit or a rat there, I would have killed it. "I would smash its head on a rock and then I would tear it open and eat its raw flesh because there would be juice in it," I thought.

It was then I realized what the survival of the fittest is really all about. It seemed right that a rabbit die in order to give life to my body since I was a higher being in the scale of evolution. My body deserved to be preserved over his. Just the size of my body in comparison to his almost ensured its superiority if by my wit I could overcome the rabbit's speed. In essence, I felt, all bodies are one, but some must die to give life to others. I felt the rabbit would understand, for he must sense more directly than I the nature of things.

As it turned out, however, there not only were no snakes or rabbits, but there didn't seem to be any life whatsoever. It was deadly silent in the canyon, and though I kept yelling "Help us, help us!" I didn't hear any answers—not even from Jim. This made me think that he must have gone to sleep.

Each time I lay down to rest, I called out, "Help us, help us, help us, somebody!" Sometimes I would add to that a cry of "Shalom! (which means "peace" in Hebrew and is used both as a greeting and as a farewell) Israeli Army! Salam Alaikum (which is, as Jim and I had learned, the Arab way of saying "Peace be with you")." The only answer was the echo of my own voice in the canyon.

I remember thinking what a strange thing it is that people talk about man's will to live when facing death. I had an overpowering feeling that it was not the will to live that kept me going. I had absolutely no fear of death, and there seemed to be such a fine line between life and what we call death that it was certainly not the will to keep my body alive which made me go on. In fact, if I had been there alone, to have gone on under such terrible circumstances—making my body get all cut up and bruised and torn and wounded in order to help *it* survive —would have seemed foolish and almost self-contradictory.

I knew that I would live even if my body died. But I was asking my body to do me a favor, not because of my own desire to survive but because I wanted to get help for Jim. And so my body was helping to carry me until I could get help for his. It was a will to live for someone other than myself that kept me going. I had no fear of death to make living seem an urgent necessity, but I did have a will to survive in order to get help for Jim.

I thought about the many stories I had heard about persons who, when faced with death, have their whole life flash before them as though in review. This didn't happen to me at all. My thoughts were about the immediate circumstances in which I found myself and any flashes of memory were directly related to my existential situation. That's not to say I had no insights. They came in abundance.

For example, while resting once I got an image of the whole of life as a big spider web. I was just one of the millions of little strands which held the web together. If I were to have given up, to have lain there waiting to die, I would have weakened the whole web. And especially affected would have been Jim, whose life was so directly connected to mine and therefore more immediately dependent on my will to go on living than most people's.

To lie there and await death would have been easier than going on, but I would have done an injustice to the entire interlocking web of life, in which strength generates strength and weakness creates weakness. And more important, I would have done an injustice to Jim, who loved life so intensely and gave all he had in each existential moment for the benefit of others and the cause of truth. I could not weaken the web.

From time to time I could hear rocks move, and then a rockslide of small or large proportions would begin. Each time I hoped the movement indicated something or someone alive was nearby. I would call out, "Help us! Shalom!" But there was no answer. Only the echo.

I became aware of the stars overhead, and of the Milky Way, which arched from one side of the canyon to the other. I thought, "If only I knew something about the position of the Milky Way at this time of the year—or about any of the configurations of stars—I could tell what direction I am going or what time of night it is."

I realized why it had been so important to people of ancient times and cultures to know the sky. Without mechanical devices, it would be the only way to keep a sense of orientation in time and space.

Finally, I came to a place where I could see that it was impossible to go around the next jutting cliff. I could see the silhouette of a sheer wall against the sky. It was straight up and down—impossible to pass. I knew then that I had to climb out of the canyon. I didn't see how I could do that, for I was utterly exhausted.

The dehydration of my body was such that I realized I would have to remove my contact lenses. There were no more fluids in my eyes to hold them in place, but I hated to take them out because I felt I needed to see as clearly as possible. In the end I had no choice. I was able to catch the right one and tuck it down into my bra. The left one fell among the rocks.

I rested for a long time and then began to say to my body, "We must climb out. If you can climb for five minutes—just five more, I'll let you rest." Then to my arm muscles: "Please lift me up to this next level." Each time a strength filled me and I was able to go on. It seemed almost a miracle; my body managed a nearly impossible task.

Finally I began to say, "Only three more tries . . . just two more now . . . maybe this time we can make it." The power flowed in from around me, for my own strength was completely spent. In some incredible way I made it, climbing out onto the rim of the canyon. Ahead of me were Bedouin grazing lands: I could see the droppings from the animals. A bright moon lighted the hillsides and I could see the brown stubble on which the Bedouin animals grazed.

A surge of joyful elation filled my whole being. I cried

aloud, "I will make it now—I will be able to bring you help, Jim." Again, into the night, I hollered, "I'm coming soon, darling. I will bring help. It's OK, Jim. I can help you now. I will bring help."

My voice trailed off into the night. I looked at my watch. It was shortly after midnight. I had been climbing in the canyon for about six hours. I concentrated hard, trying to send ESP messages of assurance: "I'll be back, my darling. I'll be back with help."

## SHALOM, SHALOM

I calculated the sun would be up about five o'clock in the morning and the heat would then intensify. It had not cooled off significantly after sunset and I continued to perspire heavily through the night. The intense heat of the day, which was about 130° on Monday, was stored in the rocks and preserved in the ground almost as in an oven. Moreover, there were no winds or air currents to cool the air, and the Dead Sea—because of its high mineral content—contributed nothing to lend relief. Nevertheless, the fact that there was no sun reduced the direct impact of the heat, and that would begin to change at dawn.

So I told my body, "We have five hours to walk. We must walk all night." I started off across the hills toward what I still believed to be the Dead Sea near Qumrân. In comparison with climbing on the canyon wall, the walking was easy, even though the hills were quite steep and the land extremely rocky, causing me to continually twist my ankle. My body was very, very tired but at least I didn't have to suspend myself from the rocks. Nevertheless, I was able to go only a short distance at a time before stopping to let my body rest. I could tell what a price the night's travel had exacted.

It was near the top of the canyon, as I was crawling out, that I first heard a knocking sound against the rocks in the distance. It reminded me of a woodpecker, but it was a much slower and more deliberate sound, and it was against rock, not wood. The knocking had no special rhythm. It would simply begin and continue rather steadily and evenly for a long time, echoing through the canyon. I didn't know what it was or what it could possibly mean. It sounded almost human in its regularity and persistence.

That knocking sound accompanied me for hours, long after I got out of the canyon. It puzzled me a great deal and while resting I would listen intently to it. It was always ahead of me, not behind me, so I had no sense that it was Jim. But once it did occur to me that it might be Jim, Jr.[1] He had on occasion seemed to be able to use knocking sounds in the house to get Jim's attention or, apparently, just to make his presence known. "He might be wanting to tell me he is here and is helping all he can," I thought.

From the hillside where I was resting, I called out toward the canyon, "Is that you, Jim?" meaning Jim, Jr. There was no interruption in the knocking; it went on in the same steady manner. Since there was no special rhythm to it or response to me, I felt it must not be intended for me. But it was a strange sound. I kept imagining a Bedouin chipping or pounding rocks in a cave while he sat through the desert night.

It was also just before I climbed out of the canyon that the thought occurred to me to drink my own urine. Feeling very much that my body was a loving friend, I

[1] Bishop Pike's oldest son, James A. Pike, Jr., took his own life in February of 1966. The story of his apparent attempts to communicate with his father during the two years following his death is told in detail in *The Other Side,* by James A. Pike with Diane Kennedy, New York: Doubleday, 1968. The author shared in a number of those experiences of apparent psychic communication during 1967 and 1968 and collaborated with the Bishop in writing *The Other Side.*

remember squatting on a very narrow place on the ledge, putting my hand down to catch the urine, and asking my bladder, "If you will give me just a little water, I can refresh myself."

Never had I asked my bladder to respond so directly and precisely to my needs, and it was slow to do so. But reluctantly it gave me a little at a time. I caught it in my hand and wet my lips with it and the inside of my mouth. It gave me a little more and I put it in my mouth. A little more, and it was enough to drink. Still more: I caught all I could, drank all I could. When the bladder was unable to give me any more urine, I licked my hands and then rubbed the remaining dampness all over my face. The whole experience was very refreshing. Finally, I licked my arms to use whatever perspiration was on them.

It seemed ironical to me that whereas in other circumstances it would never have occurred to me to drink urine—rather I would have found it repulsive—here it tasted refreshing. There was nothing bitter about it, nothing that upset my stomach. It only brought relief from the dehydration and heat.

And I felt somehow that it was right that the body should supply its own needs under such circumstances. That my bladder should provide moisture to run through my body's system when there was no other fluid available—that my own urine should provide refreshment which would serve the same function again at a later hour—seemed somehow the way of the universe. It seemed right. I felt as though one of the secrets of life had been disclosed to me. It seemed beautiful.

I was able to find refreshment in this way four or perhaps five times in the course of my ten-hour walk—nearly all of it during the last five hours, for the idea occurred to me only after I was desperately thirsty. It was not a great deal to drink, but enough to wet my mouth for a time, to get momentary refreshment. After each such occasion I tried to keep my mouth closed tightly so that it would not dry out as I walked along.

The walk over the hills seemed eternal. I had felt such joy at first, and such certainty about being able to find help. But each time I reached the crest of a hill, hoping against hope that I would see the Dead Sea, there seemed to be an endless stretch of hills ahead and my spirits would fall.

Around 1 A.M. I caught sight of a low-hanging bank of clouds on the horizon. I knew they must be over the Dead Sea, as I remembered such formations from the year before. I felt confident I was headed in the right direction, but my progress seemed incredibly slow.

It was during that long walk that time began to stretch out for me, making each minute, though filled to the brim with emotion and experience, last as though it were an hour. Time as I was experiencing it meant nothing by the clock. The watch was only helpful in relation to the time the sun would come up.

I felt as if I were suspended in eternity while possessing an awareness of the way we finite human beings mark off our minutes and our hours in order to measure our days, completely distorting the nature of eternity. Paul Tillich once preached a sermon called "The Eternal Now." I was living in it, and that aspect of the experience was to last several weeks after I returned to the United States.

Soon after I got out of the canyon, I saw a road far off to the left. Since it seemed to be headed the other direction, toward Jericho, I chose to go straight ahead over the hills toward Qumrân, knowing that there I would find fresh water and perhaps be able to get help. As I climbed up each mountain I talked to my body, saying, "You can make it to the top of that hill; then we'll know something." What I learned each time was that there were more hills ahead. So I would repeat the phrase that most persistently kept me going: "We must walk all night."

Occasionally I looked at my watch. "You have only four hours . . . only three more hours . . . till sunrise." I would remind my body, "We must walk all night."

At long last I came over the crest of a hill to see before me a road leading up to the top of the next hill, toward the Dead Sea.

"My God! A road!" I gasped. It was almost like seeing a town, a village, civilization. It was a sign of human life. I stumbled down onto the road and began to walk up it. I couldn't believe how friendly it seemed to find a road.

But in spite of my enthusiasm, I was unable to walk more than a short distance before I fell down again to rest. This time I lay with my head down the hill, hoping to get more strength and vitality flowing into my mind by having the blood rush to my head. I also felt perhaps it would rest my legs and feet if they were up in the air.

When I raised myself up again, I had to stand a long time to regain my sense of balance and to reorient myself before I could start walking. Whether the new position helped, I don't know, but I tried it several times as I walked on the road, each time feeling the same initial disorientation upon standing up.

When I reached the top of the hill, climbing on the road, there at long last was the Dead Sea spread in front of me. I felt a great sense of relief, but I could not figure out what road I was on. To my left I could see the lights of Kallia, a little community on the northwestern bank of the Dead Sea. I had some recollection of a road that went to the north of Qumrân which went directly across the desert to Jericho, but whether the road I was on would connect up with that, I could not be sure.

I knew, however, that I did not have enough strength to walk to Jericho—or even to the main road to Jericho. I therefore reasoned that if I could find my way to Qumrân, which would be to the south, I would be able more quickly to find fresh water. I shouted, just to be sure I still had my sense of direction. The echo confirmed that the wadi was to my right, the south.

I started down the road, since it was headed in the right direction, thinking that if it branched off to the left I could go across the hills to the right. I strained my memory to remember what the land to the north of Qumrân was like. I couldn't recall in detail, but it did seem there might have been a shallow wadi. When I tried to bring the scenery around me into focus, however, I couldn't locate anything familiar.

How could I get to the water at Qumrân and to the army camp nearby? I saw what I thought was the back of the Qumrân caves, but to get there I would have to cross a deep ravine and climb another precipitous cliff. Moreover, I couldn't make out the monastery on the flatlands below the cliffs. The coloration of the land seemed right, but I could see no buildings or any signs of habitation.

The moon was behind the clouds as often as it was out now that I was near the Dead Sea, so I could not always see clearly. Moreover, having removed my contact lenses, my distance vision was not the best.

When the road I was on turned to the left I followed it a short distance. Then I thought I could see it going endlessly along the sides of the cliffs to the north. "Oh, my God, no," I thought. "I *can't* walk all that way to Jericho." I collapsed on the road. Soon I pulled myself over to the side of the road where I could see down the cliffs to the flatland below, which stretched out to meet the shore of the Dead Sea. I lay on my stomach, studying the situation.

I felt a sense of desperation. It was now about 2:30 in the morning and I knew I couldn't walk all the way to the main road to Jericho before the sun came up. It was just too far. I felt I needed to make a decision, an important decision. Looking toward what I thought was Qumrân, I hollered to see if I could hear my voice echoing in the canyon. I could no longer hear it. I knew I was heading to the north, away from the canyon.

After what seemed an interminable period of indecision, I concluded I just couldn't go on the road. Instead I would go to Qumrân. I retraced my steps till I got to the first bend in the road. There I lay down on my stomach again, my head up on the edge of the cliff, to survey the terrain below and plan a course of travel.

I was so exhausted it took all my energy just to concentrate. I could see the cliffs were like the ones in the main wadi: steep and covered with sharp rock. I knew climbing down into the ravine and out again would take a great deal of strength, and once at the top of the mountain I would have to climb all the way down the other side in order to reach the Qumrân monastery.

I tried hard to keep things in perspective, to assess my strength and to make the right decision. Because I knew there was water at Qumrân, and because I knew I could not reach the main road to Jericho by sunrise, I decided I would climb through the ravine.

I dragged myself to my feet and started down the side of the mountain. At once I was again on sharp, jutting rocks, and soon I was climbing down a cliff. I rested periodically, but before I had gone too far I came to a kind of ledge where in order to go on I would have had to drop myself down a long, long way—perhaps twenty feet.

Exhaustion and desperation set in again and I lay back on the cliff thinking, "What can I do? What *can* I do? If I drop myself those twenty feet and then find I can't go farther I will really be caught. I haven't the strength to pull myself back up to this ledge. But if I go back down the road, then it's an *endless* road and I haven't the strength to go that distance either."

Finally, after another long period of indecision I reasoned that it was better to be on the road when the sun came up than to be down in the ravine. There was at least a chance that someone would travel the road in the morning and discover me there. There was almost no chance I would be found in the wadi. So with great effort, I climbed back up the mountainside and onto the road again. It took me a long time because the climbing was quite difficult and my exhaustion more complete all the time. When I reached the road, I thought I couldn't possibly go on. It was now about three in the morning.

After what seemed like a long rest, I urged my body on. "Two more hours," I said. "We must walk all night." It took a while to regain a sense of balance, but then I tried to concentrate on my feet. I would say, "You must walk all night. You must keep walking and walk all night."

My feet would place themselves down carefully, trying to avoid rocks, but it was an impossible task. The road was full of large loose rocks and the bed was soft clay dust. Each time my feet would step they would hit a rock. I would twist my ankle, cut my feet, stub my toes. Only the soles of my feet were protected by my thong sandals and even they were covered with blisters by now.

It occurred to me once that I might not be able to go on

walking if my sandals were to break, but I only let the thought pass through my mind; I didn't dwell on it.

Even with the concentration on my feet, my telling them they must walk all night, I couldn't go very far before I would again collapse on the road, needing to rest. I would set myself goals, like walking to a bend in the road, but I couldn't always make them before needing to rest again. But I did keep going, somehow, slow as my progress seemed.

I watched the lights at Kallia and kept crying out, "Help me! Shalom! Salam Alaikum! Israeli Army!" hoping that someone would hear me. The longer I walked, the closer the lights seemed to be, and I began to think, "How strange that no one hears me. This country is at war, so they *must* have army sentinels out. How is it that they can't hear me?"

I later learned that those lights were more than thirty-five miles away at the northern end of the Dead Sea. Because there is no moisture in the air, distance is completely distorted in the desert. So just as my sense of orientation in time slipped away, I also lost my ability to judge distance. To have the time/space continuum lose its hold is indeed to experience the eternal now.

Once or twice it occurred to me while I was lying in the road that perhaps I should try just rolling down the hill, using my body weight and the force of gravity to carry me. I tried it once, but rolling over big rocks cut and bruised my whole body, so I gave it up and told my body it would have to walk.

There were two or three places along the road where there was very fine clay dust completely devoid of rocks. When I lay down in that dust it felt like a feather bed. It was beautiful. I moved my arms back and forth in the feather dust and relished the feeling of luxury. The temptation was just to stay there.

At length I came to a slope which seemed to lead to the bottom of the hill. At the bottom it looked as though there was another dry creek bed, or ravine—perhaps even a canyon—and more hills on the other side. It also seemed that the road I was on continued to the left of the crevice. As hard as I tried, however, I could not bring things into focus: the moon was behind a cloud and I was exhausted beyond belief.

I could hear noises of some kind on the other side of the wadi ahead, but I couldn't tell what they were. Once I thought I was hearing cars running on a road. Then I listened more closely and decided it couldn't be cars. Whatever the noise was, it seemed to be coming from the other side of a canyon.

The fact that there was apparently a wadi between me and the Dead Sea and that the road seemed to continue on the wrong side of that canyon, going on endlessly, so completely discouraged me that I lay down in the road and began to roll. I was so utterly exhausted I thought I would just roll till I could go no farther; then I would wait to be found someday. Once in a while I had to stop to align my body with the road so I would continue to roll, but for the most part my body weight kept me moving. I tried to protect my face by stretching my arms up over my head, but I knew the rest of my body was being cut and bruised. It seemed the only possible way to go on.

When I rolled to a stop at the bottom of the road, I thought I would make one last effort to get someone's attention.

"Help me," I called desperately. "Shalom!"

A cry came back. "Shalom!"

## NOWHERE TO BE FOUND

"Shalom, shalom!" I cried in disbelief. "Oh, help me! Bring me water. Shalom!"

"Shalom," was the response again. Then I could hear many voices talking, as though debating what to do. The voices seemed to be coming from across the crevice I had seen.

"Please," I said desperately. "Do you have water?" Someone spoke and I thought I heard some Spanish words. "Hablan Español?" I asked, frantic for an opportunity to communicate. I couldn't imagine why anyone would be speaking Spanish, but I was willing to try anything.

After a pause, an answer came. "Do you speak English?"

"Yes, yes," I answered eagerly. "Oh, please bring me some water." Again they debated among themselves. I couldn't understand why they didn't do something.

"How can I get to where you are?" I shouted, thinking they were across the ravine. I was still lying on my back.

The man who had spoken to me in English hollered out, "Use your feet!"

As I look back on it now, it seems a very humorous reply, but at the time it caused me to feel more desperation. I thought, "My God! My feet! *Use* my *feet!*" It seemed an impossibility. But I told my body, "Get up. You must get up on my feet just one more time."

I could barely manage to stand and I had great difficulty maintaining my balance. I tried to focus my eyes in the direction of the voices in order to see how far I had to go.

Then I heard, "Wait."

"Please," I pleaded. "Bring me some water." I felt I couldn't walk one step farther without water.

"Wait there," they repeated. I thought they must be miles away.

At last one of the men came to help me, and I recognized that he was an Arab. We crossed what was only a road under construction—not a ravine—and started up a slight incline to the Arabs' camp.

I was so weak that I asked if I could put my arm on the man's shoulder. He responded affirmatively and held onto my arm, supporting me. Though I was trying very hard to walk by myself, I realized that I was leaning heavily on him. In fact, when we started up the small embankment to the camp, he was practically having to carry me.

I was conscious of violating the customs of the Arabs and felt most embarrassed. Their women, I understand, are supposed to be fully covered: There I was in a thin little cotton dress which I had earlier unbuttoned part way up the front to make climbing easier and which was torn on the side. My face, my hair—in fact, my whole body—was filthy. Everything about my body and my appearance seemed in contradiction to Arab custom, and more than that, I was leaning heavily on a man, my body pressing next to his, and I knew this must also violate the conventions of their culture. Arab women, as I understand it, are not supposed to touch men in public and are expected to keep their proper distance, subservient to men.

I kept saying to the Arab, "I'm sorry. I'm sorry to be

leaning on you. I'm sorry." He answered with equal persistence, "You're very welcome. You're very welcome."

A whole group of men surrounded me as we approached the first tent in their camp. They had me lie down on the nearest cot while they brought some water. "Oh, please, water!" I gasped.

After gulping down the can of water they gave me I said, "We must get the police with a helicopter." I tried to explain to them that my husband was still out in the desert. They didn't know what a husband was, so I showed them my wedding ring. That meant nothing to them. I said, "A man, like you," pointing to one sitting near me. Then I pointed into the wilderness. "He's in the desert," I tried to explain, but without success.

The men tried, with their limited English, to find out what had happened. "Why were you in the desert?" I couldn't explain to them why I was.

"Are you coming from Ein Gedi?" they asked.

"No," I explained, puzzled at the question. "We were in Wadi Qumrân—we were walking to Qumrân."

"You must be coming from Ein Gedi," they insisted, seeming not to respond to the name Qumrân at all. I knew Ein Gedi to be far to the south of Qumrân and I couldn't understand why they would think I was coming from there.

Slowly I began to realize I was perhaps not where I thought I was. "Is that Qumrân?" I asked, pointing south to where I thought it was.

"No," they said emphatically. "Ein Gedi is there," pointing in the same direction. I fell into silence, not comprehending.

"How many of you were in the desert?" they asked.

"Two," I responded eagerly. "My husband is still in the desert."

"*Where* is your husband?" they asked, seeming at last to understand.

"Far, far away," I said.

"We will go get him," they offered.

"No," I answered, "we must have a helicopter. He is far, far away."

"When did you leave your husband?" they asked.

"At six o'clock." I showed them on my watch.

"At six o'clock?" they asked, unable to believe what I was saying. "How long have you been walking?"

"*Ten hours*," I exclaimed, showing the number on my fingers. "I have been walking ten hours." I had reached the Arab camp shortly after 4 Tuesday morning, while it was still dark, but it seemed an eternity since I'd left Jim. "Please," I cried, "we must get the police."

"There's no way to get police," they responded. They explained they had no telephone, no radio, no trucks, not even any animals. They were completely incommunicado.

"Where is there a telephone?" I asked.

"At Ein Feshka," they responded.

"And how far is Ein Feshka?" I persisted.

"Very far," they said, waving their hands to the north.

Again I was confused. I knew Ein Feshka was to the south of Qumrân. Where then could we possibly be?

"Then two of you must go to get the police," I said matter-of-factly. They all shook their heads no. "Why?" I queried insistently.

"We are Arabs," they explained. "If we walk in the night, the police—bang, bang . . ." They gestured with their hands and pointed their fingers as if shooting a gun. I understood. I knew the Arabs were under severe restrictions because of recent terrorist activities.

They assured me that at six o'clock the Army came and that they would take me to the police. I asked several times to make sure I had understood the time correctly. "Six o'clock?" I asked. "Are you sure *every day* they come at six o'clock?"

They said, "Yes, every day."

Though I was at last convinced the Army would come and knew I had no choice but to wait, I was concerned. I knew it would be light by then and I was afraid that Jim would awaken and find that I was not back and that he would be worried that something had happened to me —that I had not been able to get help. Still, six o'clock was early enough in the morning that I was content to wait. It would not be terribly hot by then.

The men then suggested that I move to another tent. I later learned that they had taken me to the tent belonging to the foreman of the group. They gave me a cot there to lie down on, and one of them said kindly, "We want you to know Arabs always respect any stranger."

I felt they were trying to reassure me because I seemed so vulnerable. But rather than being afraid of them, I was concerned for fear I would offend them by my scanty dress. By now I had buttoned my skirt, of course, and was trying to be very discreet. But I was most grateful for their expression of respect.

The men who spoke the best English tried to visit with me to find out what had led to my being lost in the desert. They were very kind, but they simply could not comprehend why I would have been out in the wilderness. Finally, searching for a common vocabulary by which we could communicate, I said, "Tourists." It seemed to me that would explain any incomprehensible act.

"Americana?" they asked.

"Yes," I nodded. They looked at each other, nodding in partial disbelief and partial understanding.

"What time did you leave your husband?" they asked again.

"At six o'clock," I said, pointing to my watch. "I walked *ten hours*," I explained again.

The Arabs shook their heads sadly. "Did he fall? Was he hurt?" they asked.

"No," I said. "He is sleeping. He was very tired."

Again they shook their heads sadly. Their concern heightened mine rather than serving to comfort me. I knew how critical Jim's condition was. We had to get to him quickly. It was hard to wait until 6 A.M., but I was too exhausted to do otherwise.

Other men were bringing me water and urging me to drink it very, very slowly. They asked if I would drink some hot tea. I said yes, I would like that. So one of them made some tea—the most delicious tea I have ever tasted. It was made with some special kind of herb, and later someone explained to me that they boil the tea leaves right in the water instead of just pouring water over them and that's part of what makes the flavor so good. I couldn't seem to get enough, though it did quench my thirst more than water.

Around 5 A.M. it began to get light. They asked me if I would like to wash, so I used their soap and water to wash my legs and arms and face, getting some of the dust and dirt off me. Then several of the men got out first-aid equipment and cleaned my wounds, putting disinfectant on them. They offered me a comb and I tried to get it through my hair—an impossible task because it was sticky and snarled with dirt.

I tried to rest, but sleep was impossible. They brought me some dates to have for breakfast and I ate a few. Then I asked for more tea. They were extremely kind and attentive. I visited with them, learning they were from the Gaza Strip and were part of a road construction crew. The Israeli government brought them to the Dead Sea area to work for five days on the new road being built between Ein Feshka and Ein Gedi. During that time, they camped in the desert. On weekends they were taken home to be with their families.

They asked about me and found it almost impossible to believe that I was married but had no children, and that I did not smoke cigarettes.

"How old are you?" one Arab asked.

"Thirty-one," I replied.

"And how old is your husband?" the foreman asked.

"Fifty-six."

They all shook their heads, exchanging glances and seeming to conclude something about the age difference. Then the foreman said proudly—obviously aware of his virility—"I am forty-six and I already have seven children."

I could see Jim and I were a great mystery, so I explained, "We have only been married eight months." They nodded, but were not satisfied, I felt.

And about smoking: "But *all* American women smoke cigarettes," one man said. The whole group agreed.

"I don't," I said simply. Jim would have quoted St. Thomas Aquinas: a negative particular destroys a positive universal.

About 5:45 A.M. a truck arrived bringing some additional road workers. Some of the men went to talk with them. I said, "Please, couldn't they take me to the police?"

"No," the others replied. "They have come to work. The Army will come soon."

But in a few moments those who had gone to tell the story to the men in the truck came back and said that they would take me in the truck to Ein Feshka—the oasis just south of Qumrân on the Dead Sea. They assured me there was a phone there to call the police.

I got into the truck with the two men who had just arrived and they drove me to what they explained was the main road construction camp just to the south of Ein Feshka. We arrived there about six-fifteen. They explained that I would have to wait there for the foreman of the entire road project. He would take me to the police.

"Can't you take me to Ein Feshka to use the telephone?" I pleaded.

"There is no telephone there—not any more," the men explained. "You will have to wait here."

The two men who had brought me returned to their work and I was left waiting. There were many men around and many trucks. I couldn't believe no one could take me to get help for Jim.

I tried to ask some of the men around where there was a telephone. Very few of them spoke any English, but they were able to explain that at Nahal Kallia, which was about an hour's drive from there, there was an Army kibbutz (communal living arrangement) and they definitely had a radiophone. When I pleaded for one of them to take me, they kept insisting that I would have to wait for the general foreman. He spoke English, they explained, and he would take me.

I was nearly frantic, for it was getting hotter and hotter. Even *I* was feeling incredibly weak and dehydrated, and I had had water. A feeling of desperation began to set in again. I kept thinking of Jim out there alone in that hot desert, not knowing what had happened to me. Surely *he* would get desperate. Perhaps he would even die before we could get to him. I knew how quickly a man could die in that heat.

"My husband will die," I said, tears running down my face. "Please take me in a truck."

"It's all right," one man kept insisting. "The foreman will be here in a few minutes." Every minute seemed an eternity to me. I could hardly stand the waiting.

I asked for some water. They had given me a chair to sit on, but I couldn't sit up. I leaned forward on a table, and one of the men asked me if I wanted to lie down.

"Please," I said weakly.

They put me in a shed and gave me a blanket to stretch out on. But I had no more than lain down before an extreme anxiety for Jim came over me. So I got up again, went outside and said, "Please, won't someone take me to the Army camp?"

"The foreman is coming," said the man.

"Are you sure?"

"Yes. He will be here in a few minutes."

It was about a quarter of seven by the time the foreman arrived. I had been so impatient while waiting that I rushed toward the truck as it pulled to a stop and reached the foreman as he was just getting out and before the men had been able to explain who I was. "Do you speak English?" I asked.

"Yes," was the reply.

"Please, please," I said. "We must get to the Army camp and get a helicopter for my husband. He is dying in the desert."

They seemed perplexed by my story, which I told very briefly, but they sensed my urgency so we got into the truck to go. "Do you have water?" I asked desperately.

"Yes, of course," one man replied. I had a horror of being without water for any length of time at all.

"All right," I said quietly, trying to get comfortable in the seat of the truck. I was so tired I could hardly sit up, but I knew we had to get to a telephone, so I had to keep going. If I collapsed then all would be lost.

It was an hour's drive to Kallia, where the Army kibbutz was. The men drove quickly, but we were a long way to the south. At the gate, I climbed out of the truck just as an Israeli officer pulled up in a car.

I asked if he spoke English. He did. I explained my plight, saying, "We must send a helicopter."

"Come with me," he said. I thanked the Arabs and got into his car. We drove to the barracks where the radiophone was.

Several officers listened to my story. One brought a map and I tried to show them where we had driven. "I could take the helicopter there," I said. "I could show them."

But the officers insisted on taking the information. One thought he understood, by my description, exactly where we had been. I had told them where I emerged and came upon the Arab construction workers' camp and I had told them we left out of Bethlehem by Herodium. They seemed satisfied that they knew which canyon Jim must be in.

They left to call for the helicopter. I lay back to rest on a cot in the air-conditioned room they had provided for me. It was about 8:30 A.M.

I felt certain that now everything would be all right. Having notified the Army, I was confident that all they would have to do was go out and pick Jim up. Each time a truck drove up, I fully expected Jim to come bounding into the room, rested and full of life. I listened carefully for his voice whenever a new group of men arrived, feeling confident I would soon hear it. The door to the room I was in was closed, but I could hear the activity outside.

Members of the Army kibbutz, both male and female,

came in and out of the room to get coffee. Around 9 A.M. a man brought me some breakfast, and shortly thereafter a medic came, saying he would dress my wounds when I had finished eating. Time crawled by.

About 9:30 A.M. I went with the medic to his office. By this time I had begun to have difficulty walking on my left ankle; it had begun to swell and get stiff, my trek being over. The medic cleaned my wounds and put an antiseptic on them. He said he thought my ankle was broken, but I felt he was wrong since I had walked on it all night without pain.

I walked slowly back to the room where I had been waiting. I didn't want to be a nuisance but whenever I had a chance I asked if there was any news. The answer was the same—only that the helicopter was out searching. Time seemed to stand still. Finally, about 10:15 they called me to their radiophone. It was the crew of the helicopter, saying they had been searching but could find nothing, not even the car. They wanted me to describe again where we had gone.

I told them if they would come and get me I could take them there. They asked more questions. Was I sure we had left from Herodium? What road had we taken? How far did we drive? I tried to explain, and then in desperation said, "*Please* let me go with you. I can take you there!" The man asked to speak to one of the officers.

In a matter of minutes I was told I would be driven to Bethlehem, out of which the search was being conducted, and from there I could go with the police to look. Two soldiers took me in a jeep, driving as fast as they could. We left Kallia around 10:30 A.M. and arrived in Bethlehem approximately an hour later. First we went to the police station. They said the helicopter was waiting at the Army headquarters. We drove quickly there. The helicopter had gone.

I was never able to determine whether or not the helicopter was continuing its search that morning. I got conflicting reports. I was taken back to the police station where first I was asked to give information about Jim so they could fill out a report. This I did impatiently, inquiring periodically whether the helicopter was coming to get me. They kept assuring me it was.

After what felt like a long time, I was taken to Sergeant Major Shaul's office where I was asked to wait. People came and went, all speaking in Hebrew or Arabic, neither of which I could understand. After listening a time, however, I began to hear words I thought I recognized —they sounded like Spanish, which I speak fluently. I thought they were saying Jim was probably dead.

I began to moan and cry, quietly. Immediately the men asked what was wrong. I said, "My husband will be dead. He will be dead."

"No," they explained, "not necessarily. If he has found a humid cave, he will be all right. Men have been known to survive for as long as seven days without any water or food when they are in a humid cave."

"Are you certain?" I pressed. They nodded assurance. Those words were to be repeated to me over and over in the course of the week. I took solace in them, even when the possibility seemed remote.

"Where is the helicopter?" I asked again. No one seemed to know, but they kept assuring me it was coming. I was extremely anxious during all this period, knowing it was now very hot in the desert. If Jim was in the sun, he would not be able to live, I felt sure. I knew how exhausted we had been.

At length, the officer who had taken information from

me to fill out forms came and said we were going by jeep to where I had left my husband. "No," I insisted. "We must go by helicopter."

I was so emphatic—feeling certain that was the only way to get to Jim quickly enough—that the officer left to consult his superiors again.

When he returned, still more time had passed. "The helicopter cannot be reached," he explained. "We will go back by jeep to the exact spot where you left your husband and the helicopter will meet us there."

"All right," I said. I was disappointed about the helicopter, but eager to get on our way lest more time be lost.

About 12:45 P.M. on Tuesday, September 2, we set out in four vehicles—two jeeps and two trucks—with police and soldiers in each. "Do we have plenty of water?" I asked, remembering Jim's request that they bring lots of water.

"Yes, of course," they assured me. They also had a stretcher with them.

"Can you show us the exact way?" the officer driving the jeep asked me.

"Yes, I can take you directly there."

I remembered the route we had taken in every detail—so much so that the men were amazed. I was riding in the front seat of the leading jeep. At each turn in the road I showed them exactly how to go. When there was a particularly difficult spot, I warned them. I helped them bypass the washed-out places and pointed the way they could go through big rocks without touching bottom. They were astounded at my memory—but even more so that we had been able to travel on that road at all. They asked the questions which were to be put to me repeatedly throughout the week:

"Why did you go on this road? It is *not* a road for anything but jeeps."

"You drove this road in a Ford Cortina?" Exclamations of disbelief.

"Why did you not tell anyone you were coming here or ask for directions?"

"Why didn't you take a guide?"

My answers were feeble ones, for now that I was riding with the police I could see what a foolish thing we had done. We were following an inadequate map; it looked like only a short road—the map seemed clear enough; we didn't know we were lost. The only adequate answer I felt I could give was, "You would have to know my husband and me to understand."

"Who was driving the Cortina?" the officer asked.

"I was," I responded. He shook his head in disbelief.

"You must have ruined the car," he said.

"No, the car runs fine. It got stuck," I explained again. "We could not get it to move, but there is nothing wrong with it."

After we drove over additional difficult places he said again, "You must have ruined the car—torn the bottom out. You could not drive a Ford Cortina over this road without wrecking it. This is a rough road even for jeeps."

"I know," I said, not having the energy to insist. "But there is nothing wrong with the car."

After what seemed an incredibly long drive, we arrived at the place where the Bedouin had helped us move the car. I told them what had happened and one group of soldiers, seeing the Bedouin's tent off to the right, went to question them. The rest of us drove on.

I thought it was only a short way from there to where we had gotten stuck, but in fact it was about twenty minutes farther. At last we came to the car. It was just as we had left it: all the doors were open, the trunk was open, the rubber mats and jack parts were lying near the right rear wheel.

"Do you have the keys?" they asked. I reached down into my bra, where I had placed them nearly twenty-two hours before, and pulled them out. They were entirely rusted as though they had been out in the rain for several weeks.

"My wallet is in the car," I said weakly, not really caring. A group of eight or ten men clustered around the car. One man got in the driver's seat and the others were ready to push. The motor started immediately. The men pushed and the car was at once set free.

They were all surprised it was in working order. They had been very certain we had torn the bottom out. The officer driving our jeep shook his head and said, "This woman must be a Sabra; only a Sabra can drive over these roads." Everyone laughed. I took his remark as a compliment: Sabras are native-born Israelis.

As one group of men locked up the car, carefully placing every item inside and asking the Bedouin to guard it (they had followed us there), the rest of us drove on. The jeeps, having four-wheel drives, were able to cross the ravine between the road and the creek bed, though not without difficulty. "Show us exactly where you walked," the officer requested.

So I directed the way again. The going was rough and the way much farther than I had realized. Our jeep drove all the way through the dry creek bed, retracing Jim's and my steps. The other vehicles took the road which went over the hills and only occasionally crossed through the wadi.

At about 2:30 P.M. we reached the place where the canyon began to deepen. "There's where we began to walk on the side—along there." I pointed the way. The soldiers tumbled out of the trucks and immediately started down both sides of the canyon.

"We stayed about a third of the way down from the top," I shouted. "We were walking about there," pointing to one of the men already well on his way.

The officer started our jeep again and we took off on the road to the left of the canyon. "Where are we going?" I asked.

"To the top," was his only response.

When we got to the top of the hills, the canyon was some distance to our right. We were still on the road. Then I heard the whir of the helicopter.

"Oh, please!" I shouted. "Take me with you!" I was out of the jeep before the officer could stop me, running toward where the helicopter was landing. As it came to rest, its propellers still rotating, I was rapidly approaching it, fearing the pilot would lift off again without me.

An officer stopped me, telling me to wait. I was trying hard to cooperate and not to appear hysterical for fear they would not let me go with them at all, so I waited. But I was impatient. The propellers slowed down and the pilot signaled us to bend down as we ran toward the cockpit.

"Please, may I go with you?" I pleaded.

The pilot seemed reluctant—for reasons I could only understand later—but after consultation with the police officers, they agreed to take me. I climbed in and sat on the stretcher which was on the back seat, and soon we were aloft.

As we rose above the canyon, I began to feel sick all over. I was directing the pilot, "Move to the right. Yes, it was here I left him. There, that's the spot. Oh, we've gone too far. It's back that way."

But inside I could see it was hopeless. "My God," I thought. "Could that possibly be the canyon I walked through? How *could* I have walked through such a canyon? It is impossible."

The walls of the canyon were sheer cliffs—nearly straight up and down, like a fissure in the earth which might have been caused by an earthquake. The canyon was extremely narrow and rugged with many, many branch canyons stretching out in all directions. From the helicopter we could see nothing but sheer cliffs and rocks—we could not even see the caves.

Each time we circled back to approach the area again, my heart sank lower. It was impossible to find Jim in that canyon. We could see nothing but rocks, and the wadi was so narrow the helicopter could not fly down into it. And even though the place I had left Jim was in the more shallow part of the canyon, he was not there—or at least not that we could see. Had he still been on the uncovered rock where I left him, we could have seen him, but he would have been dead. It was now 140° and the sun had been shining intensely for nearly eight hours.

"My God, my God," I thought. "What a desolate place."

At once the thought was blotted out, however, with an influx of feeling: "No, not desolate. Barren, yes. Forbidding. But not desolate. It is filled with a strange beauty and with courage and strength. It is filled with the power of God." Momentarily I felt the calm and peace which had filled me through the night. There had been strength available for my needs—I had not been left alone.

Now, however, my concern was for Jim. I was aware of our inability to help him in that deep canyon. Certainly the same Power which had sustained me would have been filling Jim too. But *I* could do nothing. I had told him I would get help. The help was available, but we could do nothing.

As we skimmed over the top of the canyon, I thought I saw a turquoise-green pool. "That looks like water," I shouted. The men nodded. But it was so far from where I'd left Jim, and so deep in the canyon, I felt sure he could not be there. I didn't even suggest the possibility to the pilot.

After several trips over the canyon, we glided quickly out toward the Dead Sea. "That's the road I walked down," I said, pointing below us. "And there's the workers' camp."

The helicopter came to rest near the camp. As the Arabs ran toward us, I waved and shouted "Shalom!" I felt as though they were old friends; it seemed years since I had left them that morning. The pilot got out, holding his gun.

"Please," I shouted to the pilot. "They were so good to me." I didn't understand what he was going to do. The other pilot explained that it was standard practice these days to carry a gun when among Arabs. You never knew when infiltrators had made their way in among them, he said.

All the Arabs lined up not far from the helicopter and took out their identification cards to show the pilot. Having made certain they were all part of the road crew, he questioned them about me, confirming my story. We were soon airborne again.

After one more quick flight over the canyon, the pilot put the helicopter down near the vehicles belonging to the search party. They asked me to get out. "Oh, please, I want to search with you," I pleaded.

"We want to take two men who can help us to search both sides of the canyon," they explained. "Their eyes are trained."

I reluctantly got down, knowing I would only be a burden and could be of no real help. I felt sick inside. How could it be that I had been able to get help and we could not find Jim?

The helicopter took off, and I waited with the few men who were manning the jeeps and trucks. Around 4:30 the police and soldiers climbed out of the canyon and the officer in charge explained that we would have to abandon the search for the day as it would soon be dark. Early in the morning, he told me, they would start out with fresh troops to search again.

We drove to the Dead Sea and down the road I had walked. It was a severe road with many switchbacks and hairpin curves. I hadn't realized how steep it was when walking it. I thought it was because of my weakness that I could go only a short distance at a time without collapsing. Now I could see that under any circumstances it would have been difficult walking—the road was steep and the rocks and clay dirt loose, offering no firm footing for anyone. The jeeps had to be driven in four-wheel drive and even then the drivers had difficulty.

When we got down to the Arab camp, the police again stopped to talk to the workers. I waved a friendly hello, glad to see their response. I hoped they didn't think I had told the police anything false about their treatment of me—they had been so kind. The police checked all of their identification cards once more and then asked them to reconfirm my story.

Soon the helicopter joined us there and two of the police officers told me they would take me to Jerusalem in the helicopter so I would not have such a long ride. I thanked them, and we climbed aboard. Soon we were aloft and the trip to Jerusalem took only a few minutes.

Once there, the two officers took me to the hotel in a

police jeep. As we drove through the streets of Jerusalem, I had the agonizing experience of thinking that every man I saw on the street—except those in Arab dress—was Jim. Momentary thoughts would give a flicker of hope: perhaps someone found him; he's made his way out; there he is. Then we would get near enough to see the men clearly, and a terrible feeling of disappointment would settle over me. The same experience happened so many times I thought I couldn't stand the pain.

As we arrived at the Intercontinental Hotel, I realized I must look a wreck and that everyone would want to know what had happened. "Please, if you would be so kind as to come in with me," I said to the officers. "I don't feel I can explain to them at the desk. If you would be good enough to tell them what happened." It was nearly 6:30 P.M.

The officers went in with me, but delayed so long at the desk while I stood waiting that I finally walked over and asked for my key. The assistant manager of the hotel was nearby and he came over and spoke to me quietly.

"I am so sorry, madam. If there is anything at all I can do for you, please ask." I looked into the man's eyes—they were deep and soft and kind. He understood.

"Thank you," I murmured. The man at the desk brought my key and as he handed it to me I could read the silent sorrow and compassion in his face. Such depth of kindness so immediately apparent. I was deeply moved.

Then I started toward my room, thanking the officers as I left them. Other hotel guests walked by me, looking in astonishment at my condition and commenting to one another, "What do you suppose has happened? My goodness!"

When I closed the door behind me, a wave of desperation hit me. Sobs and tears tore at me, causing my whole body to shake. Then I jarred to awareness: "I must call the family before the news reaches them over the radio." I lifted the phone and placed the call. Then I remembered our dinner date with Professor Shlomo Pines, also of Hebrew University, and his wife for 7:30 that evening. I asked the operator to get me his number.

"Professor Pines? This is Diane Pike calling." I spoke with studied composure. "My husband and I had a date with you and Mrs. Pines for dinner tonight and I'm just calling to say we won't be able to make it. Something terrible has happened." I briefly told the story, managing not to lose control. "Would you be good enough to call Professor Flusser and explain what has happened?" I went on. "We were to have had dinner with him and his wife last night."

"Yes, yes, of course." Professor Pines' voice reflected his shock and concern. "Flusser called me this morning," he said. "He was worried and wondered what had happened."

"I would be grateful if you would call him and apologize for us. Thank you so much."

Professor Pines was almost unable to speak. "I'm sorry," was all he could say.

"Thank you," I said, putting down the receiver.

Again I broke into racking tears. Then the phone rang. I quickly regained my composure.

"We have your overseas call, madam. Hang on, please."

I glanced at my watch. It would be 9:45 in the morning in California. Mother would be home alone. My thoughts raced back to the summer when my oldest brother and his wife lost their first baby. Mother and Dad had returned from the funeral and had sat down to share the experience with my other two brothers, my sister and me. I had never seen my parents so shaken. Mother wept as she tried to explain, "You suffer once for yourself and once for your children." I have never forgotten those words and I hated now to put this great burden on Mother alone. Yet I had to call.

I heard her voice. "Who's calling?" she asked.

"The call is from Tel Aviv, Israel," the U.S. operator explained.

"Mother," I cried out frantically.

"Diane, what is it?"

"Mother, something terrible has happened. Jim is dead."

## DON'T GIVE UP HOPE

"Dead?" Mother's voice registered her astonishment. "Honey, what happened?"

"He's lost in the desert," I sobbed. "We can't find him." I thought my heart would break and I could no longer hold back the frantic sobs and the flood of tears. I must have given an explanation of sorts. I remember Mother asking if she and Dad should come to Israel. I said no, there was nothing they could do and that I would be coming home immediately. The police would go on with the search but it was hopeless.

"Don't give up hope, Diane. If they haven't found his body there may still be hope," she tried to reassure me.

A flicker of hope struggled to break through my despair. Then I remembered why I was calling. "Mother, it's terribly important that you call the family before they hear it on the radio. I'm so worried about Jim's mother. She has nothing to live for but Jim. Please call Gertrude and ask her to have the Downings go out and tell her—to be with her when she hears. And Jim's children must be told—Gertrude has their numbers. Call right away. They must know before the press gets it. It will be in your evening news, I am sure."

Mother assured me she would call right away, but suggested she just tell them what had happened and not say he was dead, since they had not found his body. I agreed. Then she told me to see a doctor and get sedatives so I could get some rest. I had not thought of a doctor, but I said I would and hung up.

My whole body shook with new hysteria and tears. I could do nothing but sob and cry out at the walls. "It can't be! How could such a thing happen?" I would be engulfed by a wave of remorse, crying out, "I left him *alone* in the desert. Oh, God!" I so wished I had stayed there to die with him. Then another wave would come over me of disbelief, frustration and distress. I had gotten help but, *"We couldn't find him!"* My anguish was more than I could bear.

I began tearing off my already torn dress. It was filthy and I threw it into the wastebasket. Then my bra. Inside it was a tube of lipstick which I had tucked in there thinking I might eat it if I had to, and my contact lens, which, though covered with dirt and grime, had made it the whole way.

The sobs still shook my body as I debated what to do with the bra. I finally decided to throw it away too, feeling I would never have strength again to wash it. Third, I sat down to take off my sandals. By now cuts and blisters had dried, sticking to the sandals, and my left foot was so swollen I could hardly get the sandal off. When finally I managed, I forced myself to get under the shower, hoping it would calm me down.

The shower did help, and I was aware as I washed how many scratches and deep cuts I had all over my body—especially on my feet, legs, bottom and hands. I decided my mother was probably right about seeing a doctor, so I climbed out from under the shower, went to the phone, spoke with the assistant manager, Mr. Alfons Petfalski, and asked if he would be good enough to arrange for a doctor to come and treat my cuts and wounds. He said, "Certainly."

He soon called back to say the hotel doctor would come, but if I was able to go to his office, the doctor felt it would be better since he had no way of anticipating just what he would need to treat me. I agreed to go, and Mr. Petfalski arranged for a car to take me.

The driver took me to the office of a Dr. Scherer, whose native language was English. As he treated my wounds he commented, "I've never seen anything like this," meaning all my cuts, scratches and blisters. He used an entire bottle of Mercurochrome and part of another in disinfecting my wounds.

He covered as many as he could and wrapped my left foot with an elastic bandage. After giving me tetanus and anti-infection shots, an injection to prevent bruising, and a sedative to help me sleep, he gave me instructions to see him again the next day.

Shortly after I returned to the hotel, Miss Margaret Barnhart (Peggy, as she suggested I call her), an American consul in Jerusalem, called and asked if she might come up for a moment. I said, "Surely." A very pleasant, soft-spoken, gentle woman, she said she had just gotten word of what had happened and wanted me to know she was there to help in any way she could.

I warmed to her immediately. She was genuinely open and easy to relate to. I could think of nothing she could do to help, but she noticed my swollen feet and the condition of my sandals. "Would you like me to try to find you some sandals to wear?" she asked.

"That would be a big help," I said. "They have to be large. None of my other shoes will go on my feet."

Peggy left with the promise she would stay in close touch. I was most grateful to find one of our foreign diplomats to be so personable and helpful at a time like this.

Soon Professor Pines' wife called. She said they only

wanted me to know if there was anything at all they could do for me—if I wanted a place to stay, or anything at all—to please let them know. "We are so *very* sorry," she said.

I thanked her for her kindness in calling and explained I felt I should stay in the hotel for the time being since messages would be coming there.

Before going to bed, I called home again. My oldest brother, Dennis, answered. I was relieved to hear his voice, for it meant he had taken over for Mother. Being a flight engineer for one of the major airlines, he is often home with his family for days at a time. I was grateful this happened to be one of those times.

Den said he had called Jim's mother, Mrs. Pearl Chambers, in Santa Barbara. Mrs. Gertrude Platt, one of Jim's and my secretaries, he explained, had gone to be there with her while he phoned to tell her the news. He said he was flying down to spend the night with Mrs. Chambers. He also said he had called Jim's children, had talked with Jim's former wife (the children's mother) and that our whole family knew.

"What about Scott?" I asked. I knew my youngest brother was traveling across the States with some friends.

"The highway patrol is looking for him," Dennis answered. "We're trying to find him now."

Mother was on an extension phone and said, "You sound calmer now. Did you see a doctor?"

"Yes. He gave me a sedative and I'll take another one now to go to sleep." Assuring them that I would call again the next day, I said good-bye again. I was so grateful to be able to be in immediate contact with my family.

I guess I must have slept some that night, though I remember being very restless. At 7:30 in the morning Major Givati of the Bethlehem police called and said that he was sending an officer to get me to take me to Bethlehem. I said I would be ready. I ordered breakfast but was able to eat very little of it. Then I rode to Bethlehem where I was taken to the major's office in the police station.

"I thought it would be easier for you to be here than to wait in your hotel room," he explained. I was very grateful.

"The American embassy has called several times already this morning," the major commented.

"My husband is a very famous man in the United States," I tried to explain.

"What we're doing to try to find your husband we would do for any human being. It is a man's life that is at stake," the major said simply.

I was afraid he thought I was criticizing the police for not doing enough or suggesting that they should do more because my husband was a famous man. "I only meant that that was undoubtedly why the embassy was calling," I replied apologetically. "And I'm sure that all the news media will soon be here. My husband is very well known and the press always follows his activities closely."

In only a few minutes my words were substantiated by the appearance of two gentlemen from the press. Since only the top officers in the police force wear uniforms and none of the army officers do, it was hard to tell who was on "official" business and who was not. In Israel even businessmen and university professors wear sport shirts or white shirts open at the neck.

Thus when these two gentlemen entered, I did not immediately recognize them as press. One went directly up to Major Givati and the other stood back slightly. The former talked at some length and then I heard him say (he was speaking Hebrew) "Archbishop Cooke." Imme-

SEARCH

diately my ears perked up and I thought perhaps the Roman Catholic Archbishop of New York, Terence Cooke, had said something about Jim.

"Excuse me," I interrupted. "Has Archbishop Cooke said something about my husband?"

"Oh," the man said, turning toward me. "Are you Mrs. Pike?"

"Yes," I acknowledged.

"I was only trying to explain to Major Givati what an important and well-known man your husband is. I told him there are only about three ecclesiastics who are widely known throughout America: Cardinal Spellman, Cardinal Cushing and Bishop Pike. To strengthen the point, I simply said that if you mentioned Archbishop Cooke of New York to most people in the United States they wouldn't even recognize his name."

"I see," I said, settling back into my chair. Then the reporter proceeded to question Major Givati in English. I could see the major did not appreciate being bothered by the press, so after a few minutes I said, "I will talk to you if you would like."

"Oh, would you?" he said eagerly, but kindly. "I hadn't wanted to bother you."

"No, I'd be happy to," I said softly. When I first realized that the two who had entered were press, I felt that I couldn't talk to them. But then I remembered how cooperative Jim was with representatives of the news media. He always said it was better to talk to reporters yourself so they got the story firsthand. "They're only trying to do their job," he used to say. "You might as well help them do it as well as possible."

So I began talking to reporters. When the first photographer came, I refused to let him take my picture. But I thought of Jim again and knew he would never refuse cooperation in any form if he was able to give it—not just to the press but to anyone who made a request of him—and the next time I relented. I knew getting my picture was an important part of the story.

By 10:30 that morning I had given about four interviews. Then Chief of Police A Ben Schmauel came in and said, "We want you to come with us. Do you think you could show us precisely where you left your husband?"

"Yes, of course I could!" I exclaimed. "I can take you to the exact rock."

"Did you have a map with you?" Major Givati asked, holding the phone in his hand.

"Yes," I replied. "An oil company road map. Yes."

"They have found a map with a piece torn out of it. Did you tear a piece out?"

"No, but it's possible Jim might have," I said.

The major nodded, said something in Hebrew on the phone and then left the room. I followed him out into the corridor.

Soon A Ben Schmauel reappeared carrying a pair of trousers. "See if these fit," he said. "Do you have a hat?" I shook my head: again I had forgotten to bring one.

I stepped into a room and slipped the pants on under my dress. They fit perfectly. I took them off again because it was so hot and carried them over my arm.

"They are perfect," I said, emerging from the room. Police Chief Schmauel was waiting with an officer's hat in his hand for me to use. I put it on. It was too small, but it would provide protection nevertheless.

Major Givati, Chief Schmauel and several other officers were preparing to go. When we got out in front, I realized that four vehicles, loaded with soldiers and police, were waiting for us. I didn't ask what we would do or what finding the map meant to them. I was just glad to be going out. To be doing something, to be with the searchers, was so much better than the endless waiting.

Mr. David Rubinger, a photographer with Time-Life, went in the jeep I rode in and served as a very helpful interpreter for the rest of what turned out to be a very long day. I sat in front with Chief Schmauel and we followed the command car, which Major Givati was driving. I asked when we got in the truck if we had enough water. I still had the feeling I was completely dehydrated and the thought of being without water was unbearable. They assured me they had plenty, and one of the men brought a huge container of water and placed it behind my seat.

Soon we started out. As we left Herodium we took the higher road. When I protested we were going the wrong way, Chief Schmauel explained that this took us the same direction, but was shorter. It also turned out to be much steeper and more difficult than the lower road, however, and before we had gone too far we had lost one of the trucks in our party. Its brakes had gone out. We also met several trucks from the group that had gone out early in the morning to search. They had broken down on the way back to Bethlehem and the soldiers were standing guard till help came.

Eventually the upper road met the lower one and we proceeded to where the car had been left the day before. I mentioned as we went on by that I had left my wallet and passport in the car. "Yes, we found them there this morning," the chief answered. "The money was still in the wallet and everything was safe."

It was not until the next day that I remembered to ask again about them and received them back intact. By then newsmen had reported that Jim's wallet and passport had been found near the car, far away from the car, the opposite direction from the car, etc., further confusing

## DON'T GIVE UP HOPE

everyone regarding the search and Jim's whereabouts. They had in fact been mine, and there was no mystery about their discovery.

By the time we reached the place in the dry creek bed where the canyon began to deepen, I had made up my mind that I would walk from there with the soldiers to the exact spot where I had left Jim, instead of trying to drop down to the place from the canyon above. When I announced my intention, Chief Schmauel said, "Are you sure you are strong enough?"

"If I could walk for ten hours on these feet, I can take you to the rock. If we can bring lots of water along, I can make it," I said confidently.

They gave me a canteen to take with me. I slipped on the pair of pants the chief of police had given me, put on the officer's hat and started to walk, retracing the steps Jim and I had taken two days earlier. I was still wearing the same sandals, and a tall soldier walked beside me, holding my hand to give me support. With nearly every step my ankles turned; the walking was much more difficult for me than I anticipated.

I soon began to feel the intense heat, which remained around 130°–140°. I paused to take sips of water occasionally, but after going only a short way I saw an overhanging rock which offered some shade and said, "I must rest a moment."

I was afraid I might faint, I felt so weak, but I just couldn't allow myself to. I didn't want to be a burden to the searchers, and it was important that I show them precisely where I had left Jim. The soldier who was helping me opened my canteen and began to pour water down my throat. "Drink lots of water," he commanded. I did what he said. These men knew the desert well.

Soon I was able to get up and we continued on our

way. Mr. Rubinger walked ahead taking pictures. At first I objected, inwardly, to his taking pictures, though I liked him very much personally. But after I fell exhausted into another cave I thought, "People at home might just as well know what this is like. They might just as well know."

We had to walk much farther than I remembered before we came to the cave where Jim and I first lay down. "That is the cave we rested in," I said when I at last spotted it. "That is the one."

"Are you sure?" the soldier asked.

"Yes, I am sure."

Twice before I had commented when pointing at other caves, "That might be the one, but I don't think so." When I saw it, I knew.

"From here we walked only a short way before we rested again," I said confidently. But as we went on, I could not find the rock. Ahead I could see the rectangular cave high up on the mountain that I had thought was one of the Qumrân caves. I remembered urging Jim on with confidence when we saw that cave.

"Perhaps we went farther," I said, feeling doubtful. "It didn't seem like we walked so far." As I look back on the experience I realize that Jim and I must have climbed for at least half an hour after leaving the cave and now my feet were much sorer and I was even more exhausted than I had been then. No wonder this seemed like such a long walk.

I began seeing flat rocks like the one on which I left Jim. "It could be that one, but it seems like it was up higher," I said, pointing to one flat area. We walked on. "That could be it. No—it was not so large."

I looked all around. "Perhaps we went a little farther," I said, not really believing we could have walked so far. As we rounded the next cliff, I saw the rock.

## DON'T GIVE UP HOPE

"That's it," I said, climbing up on it. "Yes, this is the place."

"Where did you try to climb up?" the soldier asked.

"Over here." I showed him the area where I had tried unsuccessfully to pull myself up the rocks. Then, turning, I said, "And I climbed down there."

"That's too steep to climb down," the soldier said matter-of-factly.

"I did," I insisted. "I climbed down there."

"No one could get down there," the soldier pressed again.

"I did," I said flatly.

"This," said the soldier, pointing to the place we were standing, "is where we found the map this morning." He had wanted to be very sure I could identify the rock before he told me.

Only then did I allow myself to look up and around from where we were. "We are so close to the top of the canyon!" I gasped. Immediately I could see that had I gone around to the right instead of to the left I could have climbed out rather easily. In fact, we both could have. I got a sick feeling in the pit of my stomach, for the going was so much easier on the hills above the canyon.

Of course, there was no assurance we would have found the road or would even have gone in the right direction had we climbed out, and there was no shade at all there, but as I looked down and toward the Dead Sea I was again struck with the severity of the canyon. It was deep and narrow and the cliffs were nearly straight up and down. To have climbed to the bottom of it was foolish, but of course I did not know that since I couldn't see. It had seemed the only safe thing to do.

"Come on," the soldier said, and we began climbing

up. I was depending heavily on him for help, and just as we emerged on the top of the canyon, the thong broke on my left sandal. It seemed ironical that those fragile shoes should have made it all that way through the canyon and back twice with search parties, breaking only after I had taken the men to precisely the place I left Jim. There was really nothing more I could do to be of help. The rest depended on the men who were searching.

Having confirmed the rock on which I had last seen Jim, the soldiers and police proceeded down the canyon, walking on both sides so they could see across and into the caves. I had rejoined Major Givati in the jeep, and with those men left to guard the vehicles, we had driven farther up the canyon to wait for the searchers.

At about 4:30 P.M. the men came out of the canyon. They had found nothing, they reported, and since it was late we needed to start back down the hill before dark.

When we reached the switchback road and began the descent to the Dead Sea it was almost dusk. Ahead of us one of the jeeps overturned. Eight men jumped out, sustaining minor injuries. One man broke his leg. Since the accident occurred at the bottom of the road near the Arab construction workers' camp, we pulled up beside them to await new vehicles to carry the men. We now had two jeep loads of searchers without transportation.

Once again the police checked the Arabs' identification in case terrorists should have infiltrated. Then everyone relaxed and sat visiting. Mr. Rubinger was still acting as interpreter for me. There I learned many things. The police told me, for example, that the Arabs had explained they had been frightened of me that first night. They thought I must have been a hyena since they knew it was impossible that any human being—least of all a woman—

should come out of the desert alone at night. It is said that the hyenas sound very much like humans when they cry out at night.

Since we had to wait, the soldiers began serving the sandwiches they had brought along. Only tomatoes tasted good to me; I could eat very little. The Arabs served us tea and I drank two glasses. They told the police that they had never seen anyone drink as much tea as I did that Tuesday morning. They had found it quite amazing.

The Arabs had provided me and two of the officers with small folding chairs to sit on. Even at seven in the evening when the sun was down and it was totally dark, it was too hot to sit inside the jeeps. There was no breeze at all and once again I commented on the lack of air currents. I was reminded we were two thousand feet below sea level and that there were only a few degrees' variation in heat between day and night in the wilderness. The primary difference was the absence of the sun beating down upon you, dehydrating your body.

Over an hour passed before new trucks arrived to carry the men whose jeep had overturned. Then we began our drive back, going first to the Army headquarters in Jericho. There we paused for cold drinks, more sandwiches and cheese and apples for those who wanted them. Major Givati made a long telephone call, probably reporting on the day's search.

Then I was driven back to my hotel in Jerusalem, arriving at about 10:30 P.M. Before they dropped me off, Chief Schmauel explained that the next day they would go back to the same area and work out in spirals from the rock where I left Jim. Helicopters would drop down to question every Bedouin in the area to see if anyone had seen Jim. It was possible, they explained, that a Bedouin might have found him and taken him to care for him. Since the Bedouin have no conception of time, they sometimes keep a man for days without reporting it to the authorities. There was no need for me to be in Bethlehem until 9 or 10 A.M. the next day, they said. I thanked them for all they were doing and said good night.

I was extremely exhausted when I returned. It was that day I began receiving telegrams from the United States from friends and family sending their love and prayers. Among them was a phone message which had been passed on to me by ABC radio from Arthur Ford, perhaps the leading medium in the United States, with whom Jim and I had become acquainted following a highly publicized television program in Toronto in 1967. Arthur Ford had, on that occasion, gone into a trance and apparently had been able to put my husband into communication with his son, Jim, Jr., from the other side of death.

The televised séance, and Jim's affirmation that he believed he had on that and on several other occasions been able to communicate with his son, caused a major controversy and led many people to believe—most erroneously—that Jim had become a "spiritualist." Jim denied this, saying psychic phenomena were far from the center of his concern or interest and criticizing his accusers for denying the possibility of facts which they had not examined.

Jim and I had had a private sitting with Mr. Ford later that same year which had proved very evidentiary—giving much factual data which contributed to our adopting the hypothesis that conscious persons survive death of the body as the most plausible hypothesis to explain the data. We had had him in our home as a guest and we trusted the man's integrity implicitly. We felt his mediumistic gifts to be both genuine and reliable.

The message was that he had had a vision in which he saw Bishop Pike, who was alive but sick and was in a cave not far from where Mrs. Pike left him.

When I got to my room, I called home to report on the day's search. This time my brother Jim, the next to the youngest (twenty-two) of our family of five, answered the phone. Dennis had had to leave on a flight to Beirut, so Jim had taken over the responsibility of answering the phone and acting as a contact for the press.

Jim and Mother told me that my youngest brother, Scott (twenty), was on his way to Israel. Scott had traveled to Israel and England with Jim and me the year before, sharing with us our research in Christian origins. In the fall of 1968 he had spent four months with us in Santa Barbara, studying under our guidance on an independent study program from the University of California at Santa Cruz, receiving fifteen units of credit for his research about the early Christian era. In the spring and summer of 1969 he had worked closely with us again, leading a seminar on "The Historical Roots of Christianity" at the university in Santa Cruz and joining us again in Santa Barbara a few weeks before we left for Israel with the intent of staying on for the fall to help us put the finishing touches on our manuscript.

Before hanging up I said, "Jim, I have had a message from Arthur Ford saying he had a vision of Jim alive and in a cave. Please see if you can contact him somehow. I know he hasn't been well and it may not be possible for him to go into a trance (trance mediumship—which involves going into a kind of self-induced hypnotic state—drains a great deal of physical energy and strength from the sensitive and therefore is not advisable for a person with a serious heart condition such as Arthur Ford's) but if he is able to, ask him if he would see if he could get more specific information. Tell him there are thousands of caves. If he could tell us something more specific about its size, location, shape, etc. perhaps it could be of help to the searchers. I don't know where he is," I went on, "but try to find him. The message was from New York."

Jim agreed to try. He told me they had been receiving messages from psychics all over the country and wondered if I wanted to know about them. I said if they could tell me the things that were similar in the various messages—the elements that seemed to match—those might be helpful. He said they would do that. "Until now," Jim reported, "the main thing they all seem to be getting is that he is still alive."

"Thank you, Jim," I said. "I'll talk with you soon."

After our conversation was over, he called Santa Barbara, as I had suggested he do, to get one of our secretaries to help him find Arthur Ford. It was only minutes after they began the search that a friend of mine from New York City called Santa Barbara to ask if there was anything at all she could do to help.

"Yes," Mrs. Platt responded. "You can help us find Arthur Ford. He's in a hospital in New York and we must reach him." She explained what my request had been and my friend said she'd do her best.

She later reported that she had called a friend of hers whom she knew belonged to Spiritual Frontiers, the organization Arthur Ford helped found to educate the American public—especially persons with religious backgrounds and associations—about psychic communication and personal survival after death. She asked her friend to find Arthur Ford and in five minutes she had the name of the hospital he was in and his room number.

My friend went twice to see Arthur Ford in the hospital, but he was unable to get anything further by way of information about Jim's location or condition. His vision had come at 8 A.M. Tuesday, Israel time. It is entirely possible Jim was in a cave, or at least a covered, shady place, at that time, for he would surely have been resting frequently as he made his way down the canyon. Moreover, he would undoubtedly have been very weak, though still alive.

When I finished talking with my brother that night, I put in several calls to London, trying to reach Mrs. Ena Twigg, the British medium with whom Jim had had his first experiences of apparent communication with his deceased son. She was not in, so I tried to contact Canon John Pearce-Higgins, Vice-Provost of Southwark Cathedral, who was the Churchman who had introduced Jim to Mrs. Twigg. When he could not be reached, I tried the Right Reverend Mervyn Stockwood, Bishop of Southwark, whom I knew also to be a friend of Jim's—again, to no avail. I had hoped that one of them could reach Mrs. Twigg to see if she had gotten any information which might help in finding Jim. Since all my attempts were unsuccessful, I went to bed, maintaining my constant prayer for strength to go to Jim.

Early the next morning Peggy Barnhart called to ask if she could come over with some messages and the sandals she had gotten for me. I said that would be fine.

Peggy not only brought me a pair of plastic sandals large enough to wear over my bandaged, swollen feet, but she also brought word that the embassy had been receiving many calls from the United States, where apparently people felt the Israelis were not doing very much to find Jim. Their efficiency, she said, was being called into question.

I felt terrible about that. First, I knew that they had not only been searching, but that the conditions were next to impossible. Secondly, they were doing all they could, I was sure, and I was distressed that they should be unjustly criticized on Jim's behalf and in his interest when he had always been such a great supporter of Israel. I knew he would want every credit due them to be given.

So I gave the following statement to Peggy, which she promised to give to the Israeli press officer for release to all media:

> I have been with the search party for two days, and want to say how completely satisfied I am. The Israeli authorities are doing everything possible to find my husband. There have been hundreds of military and police out both days, working day and night, changing search parties every five hours. They have enlisted the assistance of some of the Arabs and Bedouin in the area. Four Israelis have been hospitalized with sunstroke; and one has a broken leg. One truck has been wrecked in the search.
>
> Yesterday we went to the exact spot where I last saw my husband and at 4:30 this morning they began to work out from there through the entire area. It is difficult terrain but I still hope he will be found alive.
>
> Again I want to express my satisfaction and gratitude to those who have been helping in the search.

Then Peggy asked if she could do anything else for me. I told her my brother was coming and that as soon as I got word of his flight, I would be grateful if she could arrange to have him met in Tel Aviv and brought to the hotel. I also asked her to track down some books Jim and I had planned to pick up at a Jerusalem bookstore the Monday afternoon we had gone into the wilderness.

Finally I asked if she had a car, saying I felt I should see the doctor again before I returned to Bethlehem and that I would be grateful if she would drive me there. She not only did that, but she also took me to Bethlehem.

Along the way, two members of the press joined us, hoping I would be going out on the search and they could go along. I explained I did not know if I would be going out but that they could certainly go to Bethlehem with me, which they did.

That day I wore a pair of old slacks Jim had brought along for hiking in the caves above Qumrân and for the climb to the top of Masada. Though I had not tried on Jim's slacks before, they fit perfectly. I also wore Jim's yellow sport shirt, and this time I remembered to take along a hat, Kleenex and the keys to the car, which was still in the desert. (The keys had been returned to me by one of the soldiers the day before.) For the first time I was prepared to go out with the searchers.

I mentioned Arthur Ford's vision to Major Givati and Chief Schmauel. Both were candid in saying they didn't believe in such things. "But," Chief Schmauel said, "if you can get some specific directions or instructions, we will search there. Or if you can get someone to come along with the searchers who has these talents, we will send men with him to look."

I explained I had asked for further information and that if I got something specific I would let them know. Then, somewhat hesitatingly, as I sensed what their response would be, I said, "Major Givati, many people in the United States have offered money to help pay for the search. . . ."

"It is not a question of money," he replied. "A man's life is at stake. We are doing everything we can." I had expected that reply; the Israelis are very proud and have a strong sense of duty. They would not accept money or even thanks for what was their "job."

The day passed uneventfully. I sat in Major Givati's office and many newsmen for television, radio and newsmagazines came in and interviewed me. All asked if I still had hope. I said of course I did; as long as we had found nothing, I still had hope.

The Avis people came to get the keys to the car. I forgot I had them with me, so they got them from me that evening at the hotel. I later learned that on Friday they had gone out to get the car and had driven it back with no difficulty at all. The Ford Cortina almost did better than the jeeps on the road!

I continued to feel dehydrated. On Tuesday night, after I began to take hope again that somehow Jim could still be found alive, I began a constant prayer which left my body open to God's healing power and strength, believing that Jim could draw on my strength for his needs. As I drank water, I somehow had a feeling it was more for Jim than for me. I sensed he was being sustained by the fluid from my body. That feeling continued on Wednesday and Thursday, giving me further grounds for hope that Jim might still be alive.

Around 4 P.M. that Thursday one of the officers drove me back to Jerusalem. There was no point in my waiting any longer, they explained. The day's search had yielded nothing.

When I arrived back at the hotel, Peggy was just leaving. She had left several notes for me, among them one saying Scott would be arriving in Tel Aviv around 4:30 P.M. and that someone from the consulate would meet him there and bring him to the hotel. I calculated the time and knew he would get to the hotel shortly after 6 P.M.

In the lobby, the press was waiting. I told them I would be glad to meet with them, but I preferred a press conference so I could see everyone at once. We set the time for five and Peggy said she would make the arrangements with the hotel for a press room. I went upstairs to wash and change my clothes.

Just as I was going down to the press room, a call from the United States came. It was my brother Jim, giving me the news that Arthur Ford could get nothing more than that Jim was in a cave and alive. I misunderstood and thought he meant he *still* saw Jim alive rather than that he could get nothing further after the first vision.

When I went to talk with the press, I shared that news with them, saying it gave me new hope and I felt confident we would still find Jim alive. The press asked many questions, and I felt a tremendous drain of energy. I kept drinking water, hoping that my dehydration was a sign that Jim was still alive and drawing on my resources.

The press interview was over at about 6 P.M. and I had been back in my room only a few minutes when there was a knock at the door and I heard Scott's voice.

"Diane?"

## THE SHADOW OF DEATH

I embraced my brother warmly, blinded by tears, and somehow got him into the room with his bags. Then we both broke down, I sitting on the bed and he on a chair nearby. We sobbed out our grief together for a long, long time. Then, as I could, I began slowly to tell him the story. He asked very few questions, listening with a depth of understanding which came from knowing Jim and me well.

"I felt all along I should have been with you," Scott mused. "I felt something was wrong when we said good-bye in San Jose, but because you two were so happy, I pushed the feeling aside. I just sensed I should be along."

"I felt it out there in the desert," I responded. "Once I was out of the canyon and was sure I could somehow get help, I thought, 'If only Scott had been along I could have left him with Jim. I wouldn't have had to leave Jim there alone.' I've thought of it several times since then," I added. "But there's no point in looking back now."

Eventually we ordered some dinner. Scott told me about his trip. He had first heard the news of our being lost in the desert over the car radio while driving through Wyoming. By the time he got to a phone to call home, reservations had already been made for him to fly to Israel. He told me how both Pan American Airways and the American embassy officials in London had cooperated in getting him first a passport waiver and then a new passport so he wouldn't miss his planes. Everything had worked out extremely well, though it had been a hectic trip.

Scott said that he had called Ena Twigg, the British medium, while he was in London. Scott and I had met Mrs. Twigg the year before when Jim had taken us to visit with her. We had also had a very impressive sitting with her on that occasion.

Scott said he asked Mrs. Twigg if she had received any impressions, or information, about Jim's whereabouts. She told him that several people had called from the States to ask the same question and that all she had been able to get for several days was a gray cloud. "I wouldn't want to give you any false hopes," she told Scott. "I have very bad feelings about it."

I thanked Scott for calling her, but felt it would be wrong to be overly affected by Mrs. Twigg's feelings even though Jim and I both had the highest respect for her and felt her gifts were genuine. I felt strongly that if Jim were still alive and I gave up hope, then he would really die. I knew I was closer to him than anyone and if he needed strength at all, he needed mine.

Later we called home to tell them of Scott's safe arrival. The family said there were press reports that the search had been called off. I explained it was not true and told them what the day's activities had been. I assured them the search was continuing.

Then we began making plans for the next day. Scott wanted to go with the searchers, so I said I thought we should be there by 4:45 to be sure not to miss them. We arranged for a 4 A.M. wake-up call and a car at 4:15.

When we arrived in Bethlehem, all was very quiet at the police station. We waited and waited, but none of the officers who were in charge of the search came—nor did any soldiers or policemen to go out on the search.

At 7 A.M. Sergeant Major Shaul arrived and took us into his office. I introduced Scott and said he wanted to accompany the searchers. "They did not start out from here today," was all he would say.

So we waited.

Around 7:30 A.M. two officers came in to get more information from me about Jim. They were filling out more forms. They asked if I had a picture of Jim and I gave them the one I had in my wallet. After asking for a detailed description of him—all identifying marks, size, coloration, etc.—and a precise listing of everything he had on his person, they thanked me and left to make up their report.

Scott commented that he was amazed I could remember everything so exactly. I proved wrong about only one thing: Jim had not carried his passport with him.

Shortly after 8 A.M. Chief Schmauel and Major Givati came and we were invited up to the major's office to sit. I said, "Major Givati, my family said last night that there were reports in the press in the United States that the search has been called off."

"It is not that we have called it off," the major replied, "but that we have changed our tactics. The army and police are no longer conducting the search. Instead, Bedouin trackers—men who know that area very thoroughly, every cave in the canyon—are searching. A reward has been offered and we are sure they will do everything they can to find him. They have nothing else to do and the Bedouin are very poor. They will look sometimes as long as two or three months for a reward," he said.

It didn't occur to me then that such an extended search would be of little avail. I felt reassured, and I trusted these men. Later Chief A Ben Schmauel explained again that men who live in the desert and know it well were now searching. Though the official search had been called off—three hundred soldiers and police looking for three days had found nothing—expert trackers continued to comb the area. I was satisfied with that explanation.

It was only long after all the events that I began to understand that the police did not expect to find Jim alive after three days and had, in effect, called off the search for a living man in the desert. A reward had been offered for his body.

Major Givati held court in his office that day. Chief Schmauel sat with Scott and me, explaining everything. He told us that all policemen had served at least three years in the Army and had then had special training and schooling so that they were the best trained of all soldiers. The border police were trained trackers as well and therefore were the best prepared to watch for infiltrators, saboteurs, etc.

Major Givati, the chief elaborated, was conferring higher ranks on men who had earned them and was also hearing disciplinary cases. We sat through it all, understanding nothing since it was all in Hebrew, but noting the formality and discipline demonstrated in contrast to the informality which prevailed the rest of the time.

Chief Schmauel explained that in the Army even the officers are called by their first names and that there is essentially no distinction made between ranks. The pay is the same for all—from general to the youngest recruit. Every Israeli youth—male and female—must serve two years and all receive the same basic salary. Increases are given if one is married, and for each child.

In the police force, however, ranks are more important, he went on. Officers get called by their titles, and raises in pay are a part of the reward for good service.

When the proceedings were over it was almost noon and Scott and I decided to go down to get something to eat. We told the major and Chief Schmauel where we were going.

We were joined at our table at a tiny restaurant near the police station by David Rubinger of Time-Life, who had been so kind to me on Wednesday, Yitzhak A. Sover, Director of the Ministry of Tourism, and one other newsman, all of whom had come to go out with the search party if possible. They had lunch with us and then suggested that if we wanted to ride back to Jerusalem with them, they would be glad to take us.

Since there seemed little we could do there, we went back to tell Major Givati we were going. "If we hear anything at all, you will be the first to know," the major said.

Once back in our hotel, we had some ice cream while we read the many telegrams which had come in our absence. Then we went to our room to try to get some rest. Scott stretched out on his daybed and I lay down on the double bed. Immediately I completely relaxed, opening myself to the energies around me so that they could flow through me and to Jim. But there was a difference.

I did not feel the draining there had been before. It was as if Jim was no longer able to draw on or receive my strength. I felt that the process of my being able to lend him strength had ceased. As I pondered that and rested in the realization, I said to Scott, "If only the angels could minister to Jim in the wilderness as they did to Jesus, he might survive."

I did not, and do not, believe literally in angels, but I do believe that those spirits who were called angels in the Old and New Testaments were human beings not embodied in flesh who were able to be in relationship to and communicate with human beings in this life or in this phase of existence.

In the same way I was aware that there would be spirits surrounding Jim there in the desert who could minister to him if he could only be aware of their presence. If he were unconscious or in a coma, as I somehow sensed he was, then he might not be aware of the sources of healing and strength which were available to him.

I began praying, then, for the "angels"—Jim, Jr., and others who knew and loved Jim and who were on the other side—to minister to Jim as fully as they could. It was odd that I should not have thought of them earlier. I had been asking living persons all around the world to pray for Jim in order that as much strength and energy be sent his way as possible. But perhaps because of my very Protestant upbringing—which did not include instruction in prayer to the "saints" (that is, departed loved ones or exemplars of the Faith) but only to God himself—it did not occur to me to ask the same of those on the other side of physical death.

Now I did ask their help, and as I did I had a flash of both insight and understanding and of a possibility for action. What I thought of was the manna which the Israelites had received to sustain them during their long journey through the wilderness. It was given to them in daily portions so they would not forget their utter dependence on God—even for their daily "bread."

Not long before we came to Israel, Jim had had a new insight that the Mass—or the Eucharist—was a symbolic act of remembering—just as the manna had been a reminder to the Israelites—that God is the source of all our strength and that life, and its sustenance, comes to us each day anew as a gift of grace.

The Sacraments had always had a deep meaning for Jim and were for him the means by which gifts of healing, personality integration, joy, etc. could be received, as well as outward signs that such grace was always available and was always in the process of being received. He felt they were so powerful symbolically that they communicated to the unconscious of many persons who did not consciously comprehend them.

Remembering that, I realized that if Jim was unconscious, he could still be reached by a powerful sacramental symbol. If we were to celebrate the Mass for him, while holding him in our thoughts and prayers, he might be able to receive the symbolic communication that strength and power are available from God even now, and that the "angels"—the spirits who I was confident were surrounding him—could minister to him to give him that strength.

I sat up on my bed and woke Scott. The Anglican (Episcopal) Archbishop of Jerusalem had written me a note saying that if there was anything at all he could do he would be happy to help. "We must call the Archbishop," I told Scott, "and ask him to celebrate Mass for Jim." I explained to Scott what I thought it could mean to and for Jim. I also told him I felt my strength was no longer going out to Jim, for whatever reason.

So Scott called Archbishop Appleton for me, explaining my request. "He says he could celebrate in the morning," Scott said. It was now about 4:30 in the afternoon.

"No," I said. "Tomorrow will be too late. It must be now—soon. Please. It doesn't matter who comes," I explained. "Just the Archbishop and whoever is around in the Cathedral Close will be enough."

Scott again relayed the message. The Archbishop

agreed that at 6:30 P.M. the Mass would be celebrated. We said we would be there.

Then I immediately put in a call to the United States, asking my family to relay the message to several good friends of Jim's who were priests, asking that they celebrate simultaneously to strengthen the symbolic communication.

Last, Scott called Professors Flusser and Pines, who had been so kind to us, to tell them—though they are both Jews and it was the beginning of the Sabbath for them—that though we knew this was their holy day and they might not feel it appropriate to attend, we nevertheless wanted them to know we were celebrating Mass for Jim and we hoped they would be with us in prayer if not in person.

A little later we received a call from Mr. Robert Lindsay of the Baptist Convention in Jerusalem offering to give us a ride to the Anglican Cathedral. He, as it turned out, was a good friend of Professor Flusser's and had learned of the service from him.

Shortly after six we went to St. George's Cathedral with Mr. Lindsay. A small group of persons had gathered—the priests and those who lived on the Cathedral Close plus several couples who were active Episcopalians in Jerusalem.

The Eucharist was celebrated with the Archbishop's back to us, using the unreformed English (Anglican) liturgy. It was not exactly as Jim and I would have chosen, yet that seemed entirely irrelevant. I knew the power would be communicated just the same. It was the Sacrament which would communicate.

When I went up to receive the elements, the Archbishop approached me saying, "Take, eat. This is the body of Christ given for you and for him. Your bodies and souls are one in Christ both now and forever."

I was very moved by his words, knowing that it was not the custom to diverge at all from the words of the liturgy, and especially not in unreformed celebrations. Yet the Archbishop's words were not only very personal and meaningful, but they were also a very apt expression of how Jim and I understood our marriage. Not even death itself would separate us, we were sure.

I felt a great sense of peace at the end of the rather brief service. As I turned to go, I stopped to greet Professor Flusser and his wife and Professor Pines and his daughter, who were seated at the rear. They had walked to the Cathedral, which was a long way from their homes, because they were not supposed to ride in cars on the Sabbath. They had come for a Christian service of worship on their holy day.

I was deeply moved by the profound respect and affection for Jim which their actions revealed. I embraced them warmly and thanked them. Both Professor Flusser and Professor Pines were visibly moved by the knowledge of Jim's loss in the desert. I felt very close to them in my own anxiety, concern, exhaustion and, strange as it sounds, trust that all that had happened was somehow "right" and appropriate, though extremely hard. They expressed that same sentiment.

Scott and I returned to the hotel and gathered up the messages waiting for me. One was a call from London. We both thought it must surely be Mrs. Ena Twigg, so I asked the operator to get her for me. We would be in the coffee shop, I explained, if he would be good enough to call me. As I passed the reception desk, the telephone operator called to me to come and take the London call.

It was Mrs. Twigg. "Have you been able to get anything at all?" I asked. "I tried to call you."

"Yes, I know," she said. Now she was calling because Canon John Pearce-Higgins and her husband had sat with her the night before and Jim had apparently been able to come through. She said she would not have called except that her husband and John had listened to the tape of the session three times, and a friend of hers who also has psychic gifts had evaluated it, and they felt I should know that Jim was apparently already on the other side.

"He was just on the border trying to make the transition when he came through," she said. "It was a rather difficult session, as he was confused. 'There are so many people calling me,' he said. I suppose he meant all those praying for him and trying to reach him from this side as well as those waiting to receive him over there," Mrs. Twigg went on. "But, my dear, I wouldn't tell you unless I were very sure."

"I know," I said. "Thank you."

"Will you be able to stop in London on your way home?" she asked.

"I don't know. How much time would I need in order to see you?" I was thinking how eager I would be to get home once I left there.

"Oh, I should think three or four hours at the least," was her response.

"I see. Well, I'll try to arrange it if I can. In any case, I'm very grateful for your call."

"It's all right, my dear. And I am sorry, but I felt you should know."

I hung up the phone and joined Scott in the lobby.

"She says Jim is already dead," I reported to Scott. "She says he came through last night as he was trying to make the transition. She said she wouldn't have called unless she was very sure."

"You've got to remember what Jim always said, Diane," Scott observed.

"What do you mean?" I puzzled.

"Remember Jim always said no medium is infallible —not even Mrs. Twigg. And neither is Jim—even if he is on the other side. There's no reason for us to accept what has come through Mrs. Twigg as any more valid than what has come through the many others who have sent messages. We must not give up hope now. If he is still alive, we must not give up hope."

I knew Scott spoke wisely and I listened. Deep inside I sensed Mrs. Twigg was right, yet I knew I could not give up hope, for if I did and Jim was depending on me for strength as he surely would be, then he really would die. Moreover, I still felt very certain I would know myself—directly—if he really was dead, and the inner confirmation had not yet come.

So we did not give up hope. Yet I was confused and more desperate than ever for I knew the police were not searching as before: they had done what they could. And I knew the search by Bedouin and trackers could go on indefinitely. What could I do? What *should* I do?

Should I go back to the United States? I didn't see how I *could* go—how could I ever go?—without having found Jim.

But how long should I wait? The search seemed so impossible—so hopeless.

Scott and I ate what we could, discussing the alternatives, neither of us knowing what to do.

Shortly after we returned to the room, a call came from a Mrs. Margot Klausner of Tel Aviv. She introduced herself as the head of the leading motion picture company in Israel and as the president of the Israeli Society for Psychical Research.

"I am a sensitive myself," she said. "But I have been trying to contact a man in Haifa who has often in the past been of help in finding lost persons. We have so far been unable to reach him, but we will keep trying."

"Now," she went on, "tomorrow a group of six volunteers from the Society for the Preservation of Nature are going out to search for your husband. They plan to stay out for three days. They are expert hikers. They go out and mark trails and hike for the sport of it, you know." I sensed the group must be something like our Sierra Club in California—amateur hikers with conservationist interests.

Mrs. Klausner went on. "They have been consulting with Major Givati this afternoon and are coordinating their efforts through him, but they are taking provisions and plan to search for three days."

"I see," I said, without taking much heart. I couldn't see what six men could really do out in that desert canyon, vast as it was.

"Now," she said, "I plan to do a plumb-line test with a map to see if I can get a specific location for them. I know some of the volunteers and they will take along whatever I can give them. What I need now from you is any information at all that you can give me."

I told her all I knew. If she was to be of any help, she needed all the information she could get. I was not interested at this point in testing her psychic powers, but only in getting whatever help was available in finding Jim. All other efforts had failed: the police and Army had turned up nothing; the expert trackers had evidently found nothing. If mediums could give us any help at all, it was certainly worth trying.

"I will do my best," Mrs. Klausner said. "And I will call you and let you know what I get."

It was sometime later that evening that she called back with her report. She had used the plumb-line test [holding a weight on a long string over a map and letting it sway until it stopped directly over a spot on the map, trusting that a psychic force would pull the line to the location being sought] over two maps, one large and very detailed and one smaller one, and the result had been the same both times. These directions she had given to the volunteers and they would take the map out with them.

In addition, she reported she had done automatic writing [holding a pen or pencil in her hand and letting a force other than her conscious mind move her hand so that words flowed onto the paper, apparently as a message from a spirit] and that Edgar Cayce, perhaps the most outstanding of all American mediums, who died in 1945, had seemed to come through, indicating that Jim was unconscious—in a kind of coma—and that the searchers would have to hurry. The message said that the searchers had passed over him and had not seen him because of overhanging bushes and the very small entrance to the cave. She would give all of this to the volunteers, she said.

Then I blurted out, "I just don't know what to do!"

"What do you mean?" Mrs. Klausner asked.

"I mean, I don't know whether I should go home or stay here," I said weakly, displaying my confusion, exhaustion and desperation.

"You must not go home," she said definitely.

"You think I should stay?" I asked.

"Of course," she said. "As long as anyone is searching, you must not go home."

"Thank you," I answered weakly. Then with new resolution, "All right, I will stay."

I knew it would be terrible if I started home or got home and then they found Jim and I wasn't there. "Of course," I thought, "I must stay as long as they continue to search." But my frustration and desperation at the lack of results in the search did not diminish. I felt we *had* to find Jim somehow.

When I hung up the phone I reported Mrs. Klausner's findings to Scott. "I want to go with the searchers in the morning," he said.

"All right," I answered. "I will call Major Givati and ask him."

To my surprise, the hotel telephone operator was able to reach Major Givati for me at his home. I reported to him what Mrs. Klausner had said and that she had told me there were volunteers going out in the morning and that they had been in touch with him. "My brother would like to go out with them," I said.

"Tell your brother to be in Bethlehem by 5 A.M.," the major said.

"Will that be early enough?" I asked.

"Yes," he said. "Tell him to be there at five."

Scott and I discussed it and he felt he preferred to be there by 4:30 A.M. so as to be sure not to miss the search party, so we asked for a car at 4:15 and decided to try to get some rest.

I was feeling so completely exhausted I told Scott I thought I would wait in my hotel room on Saturday and rest. "I feel somehow you will find Jim," I said, "but I haven't the strength to go along. I will wait here."

We were awakened at 4 A.M. and Scott began to get ready to go. Then at 4:15 the phone rang again. It was a call from Dr. Ian Stevenson from the United States. He said he had a message from a gentleman he did not know who said that though he had had many psychic experiences before, he had never talked about them. However, in this case he felt he just had to tell someone because the message seemed so specific and it just might be of some help in the search. He could not feel right about not passing it on.

"I don't know the man at all," Dr. Stevenson went on, "and I don't know if you want to have the information."

"Oh yes, please," I pleaded. "Anything you have and the more specific the better."

"I can give you what I have, but I don't have the message verbatim. I can get it for you."

"My brother is about to leave to join the searchers in Bethlehem," I said. "Give me what you have and then if you can get more I can try to get the additional information to them before they go out."

I took down what Dr. Stevenson had and gave it to Scott. Ian promised to call me right back with the verbatim message, which was quite lengthy. I told Scott to call me from Bethlehem before the search party left.

Dr. Ian Stevenson is a scientist and scholar in the field of parapsychology. He is Professor of Neurology and Psychiatry of the University of Virginia School of Medicine, and he gives a great deal of his time to the scientific investigation of reincarnation. He is the author of *Twenty Cases Suggestive of Reincarnation* (Richmond: William Byrd Press, Inc., 1966) and Jim and I had met with him on three different occasions and had the highest respect for him as a scientist and scholar and as a person of great personal charm and integrity. We both trusted him.

He was attending a convention of the American Association of Parapsychology at the time the news came of Jim's being lost in the desert. He had reported that they were making every effort to contact the most reliable sensitives they knew to try to get something that would help in the search.

Many persons at the convention had tried to locate a medium in Holland that they all felt might be of help. I had asked my brother Jim about the same man, and he had said Arthur Ford had mentioned him as the only medium he felt might be of help. Money had been made available by several persons in the United States to fly him to Israel if he could be located, but no one seemed to be able to find him.

Only ten minutes or so passed before Dr. Stevenson called again with the complete message. It gave specific directions to the searchers and was much more detailed than most messages, so I took it down verbatim, even though it was a lengthy message.

"I hope it will be of some help," Ian said.

"I do too," I responded. "If you get anything else at all, please do let me know. I'm going to hang up now so I can try to get this to my brother before the search party goes out. Thank you for calling."

Within a matter of minutes Scott called. "Do you have time to take this down?" I asked.

"Yes," he replied. "No one is even here yet. The volunteers are just beginning to arrive."

I read him the complete message and then said, "Good luck. I hope you find him today."

"I feel sure we will," Scott said. "Will you be all right?"

"Yes," I said. "I'm going to try to sleep."

I did go back to sleep, but at 7 A.M. I woke up feeling desperate. I was so weak I didn't feel I could go to Bethlehem, but I didn't see how I could stay in that room alone all day. About 7:15 A.M. I called Peggy Barnhart of the American consulate. Apologizing for such an early call, I explained that Scott had gone out on the search and asked if she would mind coming to be with me in the hotel.

"I'll be over in just a few minutes," she said. Not more than fifteen or twenty minutes later she joined me and stayed with me the rest of the day.

I don't ever remember being so grateful for anyone's company as I was for Peggy's that day. She was the perfect companion for me: When I felt like talking, she carried on lengthy conversations about whatever subject interested me. We talked about the conflicts between Arabs and Israelis, about the difficulties of administrating Jerusalem, about the lack of cooperation among Christian groups, about her other experiences in foreign service. I told her about Jim, his difficulties with the church, our beliefs and studies, the purpose of our visit.

When I fell silent she simply sat quietly and calmly, letting me set the pace. We ordered both breakfast and lunch in the room, as I didn't want to leave the phone or see other people. I felt sure we would hear something by late morning. When it got to be 2 P.M. I got dressed and began going to the window, impatiently watching for Scott's return.

The day seemed eternal. By about 3 P.M. Peggy began to watch at the window for me, reporting each time we heard a motor whether it was a bus, a taxi or some other vehicle. At long last—about 7 P.M.—a Volkswagen pulled up.

"That looks like Scott," Peggy said. He was into the hotel before I could get to the window, but within a matter of seconds the phone rang. It was Scott.

"Any luck?" I asked expectantly.

"We found nothing," Scott said. I didn't allow myself to feel.

Scott went on. "Diane, three of the volunteers who went on the search today gave me a ride to the hotel. I told them I was sure you would want to speak with them—to thank them for helping in the search, and to meet them. Do you feel like you'd like to come down and meet them?"

"Of course," I said. "I'll be right down."

"Shall I wait here?" Peggy asked.

"Why don't you?" I suggested. "Since you've stayed this long you might as well hear about the day's search. We'll be right back."

I hurried down to the lobby to meet Scott. He was by himself. After telling me again that the searchers had found nothing, he gave me a sketchy account of the day's search as we walked out to the car where the volunteers were waiting. He pulled a clear plastic sack out of his back pocket, explaining, "Gideon, who's waiting in the car, found the only two things all day. He found this plastic bag, but I told him I was sure it meant nothing. You and Jim didn't have a plastic bag like this, did you?"

"No, nothing like that," I replied.

"And Gideon also found some boxer shorts in a well, but I'm sure they're not Jim's. He wrote down the description from the label." Scott held out to me a piece of paper on which was written information from the label of a pair of shorts.

"Those are Jim's! Jim had on a pair just like that," I exclaimed.

We were now at the car and the volunteers stepped out to meet me. Scott asked Gideon to tell me about the shorts he had found.

"They are Jim's!" I said again. "Come up to the room and I will show you a pair like them."

The volunteers, Scott and I rushed up to the room. I

got out a pair of Jim's undershorts and showed Gideon. "Yes, they are the same," he said. We matched labels and found a pair which were identical to those found in the desert.

"What shall we do?" I asked, real hope ringing inside of me for the first time since Monday. "Should we call Major Givati?"

The volunteers looked at each other and then Gideon said, "Yes, I think we should."

I immediately put in the call. When the major was on the line, I said, "Major Givati, this is Mrs. Pike. The volunteers have found a pair of my husband's undershorts. I will let you talk to the man who found them."

Gideon went on the line. He spoke with the major for a short while in Hebrew and soon hung up the receiver. "An officer will come here," he said. "We are to wait here."

We got ice water and more chairs for the volunteers and within five minutes Major Givati, Chief Schmauel, Sergeant Major Shaul and another officer who had helped conduct the search in the desert arrived in civilian clothes and sat down to hear the volunteer's report. With a map spread out before them, they laid their strategy for the next morning.

Chief Schmauel spoke to me. "Say nothing to the press," he said. "Tell them nothing."

"Of course," I agreed. "May I go with you tomorrow?" I asked the major.

"No," he said kindly. "Your brother may join us at 5 A.M. in Bethlehem, but you may not go. If you will come to Bethlehem you can wait there with me."

"Thank you," I said. I knew he was right. I was so weak I could not really join the searchers without being a burden.

Before the officers arrived, Peggy had left to go talk

with the press. She had told them I would have no statement to make until I had heard the reports of the day's search. Now she checked back in to see if there was anything else she could do. I filled her in on the events and said I would talk with her the next day. I thanked her again for being so kind and such an amiable companion.

After Peggy had gone and I had given a noncommittal statement to the press, Scott and I called home. With great excitement I told them of the undershorts which had been found. I said I felt sure we would find Jim the next day, but I warned them not to say anything to the press since the police did not want a contingency of photographers along. Scott had explained how the police had had to go through everything twice on Saturday: once for real, and once so that the photographers could get it on film.

Then Scott got on the line. "I just want to temper Diane's optimism," he said. "We don't know what the shorts mean. They don't guarantee anything. It's just that it's the first clue we've found. We hope we will find something tomorrow. That's all we can say."

# THE END OF A SEARCH

About 9 P.M. Scott and I went down to have dinner. After ordering two minute steaks for him and one for myself, Scott had an opportunity to recount the day's search in detail. He told me that three jeeps had gone out carrying twenty men—five of them newsmen, four volunteers, Scott and several policemen. Having left Bethlehem at 6:40 A.M., by 8 A.M. they had reached the place where Jim and I had abandoned the car. Shortly before reaching the site where the Cortina had been stuck, two of the volunteers got out and started searching the ridge of mountains north of the canyon, working their way east toward the Dead Sea.

Scott stayed with the rest of the group, which drove beyond that spot and then began working their way back along the ridges—to the west—planning to meet the others in the middle. This search was partially in accordance with directions given by one of the mediums. The mediumistic message had suggested the search focus its attention on the north side of the ridge, but searchers felt the south side, which was closer to the site Jim had last been seen, was more promising. In any case, the first half of the day's search bore no fruit.

While Scott was hiking, he had seen two or three rabbits, which amazed the volunteers and the police, for none of them had seen any wildlife whatsoever in that region. Also during the morning, he had had a couple of occasions to sit and wait for his partner—one of the volunteers. He used that time for writing and shared with me what his thoughts had been.

At 11:30 A.M. he had written: "Still looking. Am sitting on top of a mountain waiting to see/hear my two companions from the SPN [Society for the Preservation of Nature]. It is relatively cool today (110°) with a saving wind. I am very tired and pretty thirsty. One cannot maintain a high level of hope when traveling by foot through such desolate country. Only my own desire to find Jim either dead or alive, the substance and strength of which is my hope to spare Diane the agony of uncertainty, keeps my spirit hopeful and my body moving. When walking I call out for Jim, saying, 'It is Scott and Diane,' for she is, I feel, very much with me. I also invoke the assistance of God (in this seemingly godforsaken place) and of Jim, Jr., and Edgar Cayce in leading us to Jim. In any case (be he dead or alive) I pray that he is now, or will soon be, in peace, which I know he deserves."

At 11:40 A.M. he wrote: "Perhaps it was willed that Jim die. If so, Diane and I join in saying 'May God's will be done.' Our only difficulty is that inherent to human pretension and impatience: Why can't we know? and now?"

By noon a new feeling settled over him, so he wrote, "We do this for Diane's peace, for Jim is at peace." He was filled with a mixture of emotions: excitement, reverence, awe and hopelessness there in the desert, but the feeling that Jim was at peace persisted after that time.

When the search of the ridge was complete, the jeeps drove on to the main wadi and again the volunteers set out. Scott spent about an hour searching in every cave he could see on the north side of the canyon, where Jim and I had walked, but finally realized the futility of that:

## THE END OF A SEARCH

Three hundred other men had searched that area for three days and had found nothing. There were thousands of caves, and he was only one person.

He had insisted, however, that the canyon should be searched again. When the police had said it was impossible any man could have walked at the bottom of the canyon beyond where the search had thus far been conducted, Scott said, "But you said it was impossible that Diane should have done what she did too. She told Jim she was going to the base of the canyon and that she would follow it all the way to the Dead Sea. He would have tried to follow her—he would have gone to find her. The base of the canyon must be searched. You don't know Jim."

Gideon Mann, one of the volunteers, agreed with Scott that the wadi should be searched. Thus he and the volunteers set out to comb the canyon beyond where the soldiers and police thought it was possible for a man to go. The rest of the search party drove to the top of the ridge overlooking the Dead Sea and waited. When the volunteers emerged after four o'clock, Gideon Mann brought news that the first clue had been found: Jim's undershorts floating in a pool of water. (It was not until several hours later that I gave positive identification of the shorts.)

I was aware of three major things for which I was most grateful, as Scott told his story. First, I was thankful for the volunteers from the Society for the Preservation of Nature. They had searched the longest and hardest that day, and had found the first clue. Second, I was grateful for the mediumistic messages I had received, if only because they were specific enough to cause the police to send out another search party. That their directions had not been accurate was not so important, since every effort had been fruitless until today. And third, I was most thankful for Scott, who, because he knew Jim so well, had insisted that Jim could have gone on—and would have out of his concern for me—past the point the police thought possible for any man. These three important factors had made all the difference in the day's search, I knew.

When we had finished dinner and returned to the room, Scott got several phone calls from members of the press who had been with him all day in the desert.

"Is it true that your sister has positively identified the undershorts as belonging to her husband?" one reporter asked.

"No," Scott replied, "she has not even seen them."

"What plans do you have for tomorrow's search?" several queried.

"I have none," was Scott's response. "Diane is going to Bethlehem at about 8 A.M. I have no plans to go at all and I don't think a search party is going," he told them.

As Scott turned from the phone, he told me, "It is the first time I ever remember telling such a bold-faced lie. It makes me feel awful, because these men have been out every day and now they may miss the climax of the story. But I guess there was nothing else I could do."

"No," I said. "We have to do all we can to cooperate with the police. They have been so good to me and have done everything I have asked of them."

I had requested the adjoining room for Scott that night, feeling he needed a good rest and knowing it was likely my phone would awaken him several times during the night. I urged him to go to sleep while I arranged for a car. He was in bed by 11 P.M. and I by midnight.

At 1:30 A.M. I was awakened by two loud knocks at the door. I leapt out of bed and dashed to the door, flinging it open. There was no one there. As I closed and locked the door and turned toward the bed again, I felt tremendously weak and dehydrated and sensed that Jim must be losing strength. I quickly got back in bed, drank a full glass of water, lay down on my back and sent all of my energy to him, letting it flow out of me.

As I did so, I suddenly saw a very husky old woman just above the right side of my bed. My eyes were closed when I first saw her, so I opened them. She was still there.

It was not completely dark in my room, as some light came in from the outside: the front of the hotel was brightly lit. But at that moment I was aware of nothing but the darkness all around and this woman's figure.

I want to describe her carefully, because I am sure this could only be called a vision and I had never had such an experience before.

All I could see of the woman was her head, her shoulders and her body down almost to her waist. She appeared to be dressed in some kind of loose-fitting white robe which hung in such a way as to cause the candle she was holding to cast long vertical shadows on her, giving the impression of both lightness and darkness at the same time.

Her shoulders were broad and husky and she was carrying a very large, lighted candle, the flame of which was almost directly in front of her face. The candle was so big she seemed barely able to get her hands around it. It reminded me of the large candles sometimes carried in Church processionals or those which stand around the communion table in Grace Cathedral in San Francisco.

Her face was rugged-looking, but kind. It was almost round and her hair was parted in the middle and pulled back off her face, as though in a bun. She had heavy eyebrows and a very warm smile on her face.

She seemed to be approaching me quietly, slowly. Behind her was another woman in procession, approaching slowly, following as in rhythm or step with the first one. Though I had opened my eyes, I could see the woman equally well and could sense the warmth and kindness with which she approached me. Suddenly I knew she was Death.

"No!" I cried out. "Please, no!"

Immediately, she disappeared, as did the figure behind her. I concentrated harder than ever before on sending my strength and energy to Jim. I knew time was very short and he could not live much longer. I was praying desperately for his survival as I fell back to sleep.

At 3:30 A.M. I was again startled awake, this time by what seemed to be voices—not actual voices, but more like those one hears in a dream. The voices were saying, almost in unison—and they seemed to be speaking from the right side of the bed, where I had seen the woman— "All of the mediums say he is dying."

"No, please," I sobbed. "It's only a few hours till we will find him. Give him strength." Then as though to Jim, "Try to live, Jim. Take my strength," I called out aloud.

Then I saw Jim. He was, as I saw him, lying on his left side on a ledge under a very large overhanging rock. His head was very near a crevice between the overhanging rock and one to the left of it which also bulged out but which had no ledge under it. The cliff from which the rock to the left hung seemed to jut out toward me, indicating that it sat at an angle to the ledge where I knew he was dying.

As soon as I saw Jim so clearly, I got out of bed and went into the adjoining room where Scott was asleep because I wanted him to share that moment with me. I walked around to the right side of his bed and sat down next to him.

"Scott," I said, touching him gently to awaken him. "It's Jim. He's dying. I want you to share this with me."

Scott woke up and scooted up slightly on his pillow, not comprehending what I was saying. "It's all right," I said quietly. "It's all right."

I closed my eyes so as to see Jim better and began to describe the vision to Scott as I was seeing it.

"He's lying on a ledge," I explained, "under a large overhanging rock. It's a very smooth rock—very large. He's on his left side. I can't tell if he has a shirt on or not, but he has his trousers on and his shoes. I can tell he has his shoes on. And he is wearing his glasses. He has his glasses on.

"I can see him beginning to leave his body now," I went on, tears streaming down my face. "His spirit is very light in color—white. It seems to be made of a filmy, almost vaporous, cloudlike substance. I can see his spirit leaving his body." It seemed to depart from the base of the neck, just where the neck meets the shoulders. His back was to me.

It was only after the full length of his body had departed in spirit form that a small trail of the same substance seemed to be left behind, now seeming attached to, somehow, or flowing out of, his head. It was shaped something like a column, fairly substantial in width but not so wide as Jim's spirit itself. The column seemed flexible, almost as though it were floating freely in the air, yet it was attached both to the body and the spirit.

"It's so strange," I told Scott. "I want to describe this exactly as I'm seeing it. The spirit is moving up through the crevice between the two rocks—up toward the top of the canyon. As it goes up I can recognize it as Jim and I can tell he is smiling, but the form has no features. It is about Jim's height, and it is more or less the shape of the exterior outline of a body, but it has no arms or legs that are distinguishable, and no eyes, nose or mouth. Yet I can tell he is smiling. And I get such a sense of peace." The tears were a mixture of relief and sadness—and a growing feeling of joy.

"It's taking him so long to reach the top of the canyon," I told Scott, "it must be a very long way up to the top. He must be far down the sides of the cliff wall." We waited in silence. Scott also had tears streaming down his face now. "It's taking him so *long* to reach the top," I commented again.

We waited in silence. The long white column continued to stretch out along the crevice, still attached to the body. It seemed less substantial now, but it was still definitely there.

"He's finally reached the top of the canyon," I told Scott. "He's pausing there a moment. Now he has started to move very slowly along the top of the canyon, right on the edge. The column is making a trail, marking just where he has been. He seems to have come to another cliff which juts almost directly back to the right. Behind him is a hill and he seems not to be able to go any farther. He is pausing there—such a long time."

"Of course he is," Scott said. "He's still looking for you."

"Maybe so," I mused. Then, "Now he's begun to move back. As he goes, he seems to collect the column with him. It no longer shows on the top of the canyon.

"He's back to where he started, almost directly above his body," I went on. "He's pausing there as though looking back the way he had come when walking in his body." It seemed strange to me to be talking this way, but it was all very vivid and real. I tried not to distort it in the least as I reported it to Scott by trying to interpret anything.

"Now he's beginning to go up in the air," I went on. "Oh, Scott, this is so strange," I commented. "Jim and I have made so much fun of ascensions and he actually *looks* like he is ascending! It's so strange to see him as though he were ascending."

I smiled. The irony was enormous. Certainly the last thing either Jim or I would have imagined for ourselves or for anyone else would have been an "ascension" in any sense of the word. Yet I was seeing just that.

"As he rises up above the canyon, the column is beginning to dissolve from the top. It is drifting away—apart, almost like a cloud when it is blown into wisps by the wind and vanishes in the sky. And his spirit keeps going up."

I had a growing sense of joy to add to the peace which I had felt from the beginning. Then suddenly I saw—above Jim—a huge crowd of people waiting.

"My God, Scott, there are *so many people* waiting for him. Hundreds of people. And this is really strange too. You remember the passage where Paul talks about the huge cloud of witnesses?[1] Well, all of these people look just like that—just like a cloud. They are more or less the same height since they are about the height of human beings, and since they are standing in a big crowd and are suspended in the air, they actually *look* like a cloud. The sky seems to be dark, but nevertheless the *feeling* I get is that of a light, billowy cloud against a bright blue sky. That's the feeling I get.

"Jim is getting up closer to them now. How strange this seems," I commented again. "There's another place where Paul is talking about the resurrection and our encounter on that day with Christ when he says that those

[1] This passage is actually found in Hebrews 12:1: "therefore, since we are surrounded by so great a cloud of witnesses . . ."

who have died before us will be raised up and we will all join him (Christ) together in the sky.[2] That is just what Jim seems to be doing: joining them together in the sky. What a strange thing." I suppose the strangest part for me was to be seeing so literally what I had supposed to be symbolic expressions of meaning.

"Now Jim is approaching the crowd. He's moving very slowly. He is so happy, Scott, and so much at peace. It's just beautiful. Jim, Jr., is standing to the left of him. He's stepping out now to meet his dad. I don't know how I recognize him, for he doesn't have any features either. But I know him. He's taller than his dad and looks strong. They are embracing. Such a warm, loving embrace. And so much joy. You should see the joy, Scott. It's just *beautiful*. So much joy."

The embrace with Jim, Jr., lasted a long time. Their bodies appeared to have completely merged into one, yet I could "see" both Jim and Jim, Jr. I could tell they were two, not one. It was a beautiful, rare moment, and it filled me with a joy approaching ecstasy.

Finally, after what seemed like a very long time—Scott and I had just been waiting in silence—the embrace ended.

"They are beginning to part now. Very slowly they are pulling away from one another—almost reluctantly. Oh, Scott, the embrace was filled with so much love and joy. I've never seen anything so beautiful." I hoped Scott was sensing the joy. I wished he could see what I was seeing.

"Jim is turning toward the crowd again now. It's almost as though Jim, Jr., is going to present him to the group. There's an older man standing to the right who is

---

[2] I Thess. 4:17: "Then we who are alive and who are left shall be caught up together with them in the clouds to meet the Lord in the air . . ."

stepping toward him now. Jim is turning to embrace him. It must be someone he knows well, for it's a very warm and loving embrace and there is much joy in it too, but I don't recognize the man at all. I don't know who he is."

I thought it might be Jim's father-in-law, Elias Yanovsky, since they had been very close and Elias had appeared to come through in several séances, but I hadn't known Elias and therefore would not have recognized him. The second embrace was also nearly a complete merging of bodies but it was much briefer than the first one.

"Is Paul Tillich there?" Scott asked, in obvious reference to the late theologian whom Jim respected so highly.

"I can't see," I said. "I can't see." Then I went on describing what I did see.

"They are parting now and Jim is turning back toward the crowd. They are opening up a way for him to walk into their midst," I explained. "It is almost as though they are opening up a corridor of air for him to move along." I watched Jim as he began to move into the group.

"There's Paul Tillich!" I exclaimed. Jim was moving very slowly as though he were trying to take everything in as he went. About the third person on his right was Paul Tillich. Though again I could see no features, I had the distinct impression that he was an older (gray-haired?) man, with a very small mustache and glasses, and though I didn't know if those features would be Tillich's, I did "recognize" him somehow. In any case, I didn't see the features; I just got impressions—a feeling tone.

"Jim is turning toward him in a most respectful way. He is reaching out as though to put his hands on Paul Tillich's shoulders. Now he is warmly but respectfully embracing him, first to the left and then to the right." I sensed a tremendous satisfaction in Jim for meeting and having a chance to greet his old friend and mentor. "Jim seems very glad for the meeting. It adds to the joy."

"Do you see anyone else in the crowd?" Scott asked.

"No one that I recognize," I responded. "Now Jim is moving on into the crowd. They are making a way for him. He's moving very slowly," I observed.

"There's Bobby Kennedy!" I suddenly exclaimed. "He's standing way back in the crowd on the right. He's not coming forward to greet Jim, but he seems to be watching him from a distance."

Jim moved on into the midst of the crowd and then, "They are closing in around him now," I told Scott. "They're gone." The crowd had enclosed Jim and when I could see him no more, they all disappeared.

For the first time I opened my eyes.

"Oh, Scott," I said, "how *beautiful!* So much joy! Nothing but joy and victory. Jim was so *happy* and so much at peace. What a *beautiful,* beautiful thing."

Scott was watching me intently. He was wide awake. "Could you draw a picture of what you saw?" he asked. I nodded, and he handed me a yellow pad and a pen. I sketched out the rocks, the crevice, Jim's body, the top of the canyon, the hill above, the trail his spirit had traced and a pool of water at the base of the canyon below. Neither Scott nor I remember my seeing or mentioning a pool during the vision, but when I drew a picture immediately after the experience I put it in.

Then I drew the crowd which had awaited Jim, putting X's where the various persons were standing. When I had finished, Scott put initials by the X's so we wouldn't forget who they were.

Suddenly the phone rang. It was the telephone operator calling to wake Scott so he could go to Bethlehem. It was 4:15 A.M.

"That experience lasted forty-five minutes," I said in astonishment. "Forty-five minutes!"

"Yeah," was all Scott could say. He seemed deeply moved by it all.

I got up off the bed and said, "I'm going with you to Bethlehem. I know you will find Jim's body this morning and I want to be along."

I was filled with joy and peace and an awareness of the victory over death which I was sure Jim was enjoying. Both Scott and I felt a great sense of relief just to know—to know Jim was dead. The knowing would have been much easier than the uncertainty even if it hadn't been such a joy-filled vision.

We arrived in Bethlehem about 4:45 A.M. The volunteers and soldiers were just beginning to arrive. When the sergeant in charge of the search came, I said, "Please, may I go along? I promise to stay in the jeep and not to be a burden."

After a moment's pause he nodded and said, "OK." I had some breakfast (Arab bread) then so I would be strong, and drank two glasses of tea. Finally the troops and the volunteers were ready. A police dog had been brought along. I had given Major Givati a pair of Jim's pajamas and his robe, the only items of clothing I had which I had not washed after he had worn them, plus a pair of shoes, which they did not think would help.

The dog's trainer rode with him in the back of one jeep. Scott and I rode with some police, volunteers and an Israeli newsman in the sergeant's jeep. Shlomo, the Israeli newsman, stayed with me nearly all morning and acted as an interpreter. He was the only person from the press who came along. He was very young—a friend of some of the volunteers. "I actually came along to help in the search," he explained. I was grateful for his company and assistance in translating for me.

As we drove along, I pointed out to Scott the exact places Jim and I had stopped so he would recognize them all. I explained each step of our journey. Scott asked questions, trying to get it all clear in his mind.

After the long and difficult drive over the road that was by now very familiar to us, we got up to the top of the canyon near the place where the first clue had been found. The soldiers, police and volunteers tumbled out of the trucks and started down into the canyon. Scott went along. Obediently, I stayed in the jeep. After a short while I got into the back of the jeep thinking I would write awhile. Scott had suggested I should make a record of the sequence of events.

When I was unable to concentrate on that, I tried resting. That was worse. Finally, I got out and started wandering around. I walked out on the rim of the canyon and looked down into the deep, deep ravine. There I could see one of the searchers—Shlomo—climbing along about midway up the side of a cliff in a side canyon. He was looking in caves as he went along, but above him and below him was cave after cave which went uninvestigated. "Look above you," I shouted, pointing to what looked like a rather deep cave covered by bushes—fitting almost exactly the description given by several mediums. But he could not hear me and the futility of the search settled over me again.

The dog trainer had asked me to open the plastic bag carrying Jim's pajamas so he wouldn't mix his own scent with ours. Then he let the dog take the scent and started toward the canyon with him. I knew that on Wednesday morning they had taken two police dogs out on the search. It had been so hot that after fifteen or twenty minutes the dogs collapsed. They could not go on.

On Sunday it was somewhat cooler—around 120°—so it was everyone's hope that the dog could be of help. But when his trainer led him to the edge of the canyon and started down the cliff with him, the dog—in spite of all his strict training—broke away and ran. It was afraid to go down such a severe cliff—it knew better and refused to go. It took the trainer nearly four hours to catch the dog again and get it back to a jeep.

In the canyon below, the search went on. The men had climbed clear to the base of the wadi and were moving among the boulders. Several of them were carrying broom handles to assist in hiking. One such stick had been given to Scott. Most of the men were also carrying knapsacks with food and water canteens so they could stay down for some time if they needed to. Nearly all of the men were carrying guns, either side arms or submachine guns.

When they came to one particularly difficult place, the border police said they would have to wait until men came with ropes before proceeding down the wadi. However, Scott found a passageway through and down some smooth boulders and the entire search party slipped down the rocks and continued at the bottom of the canyon.

By 8:40 A.M. they had reached the pool of water where Gideon had found Jim's undershorts the day before. The pool was at still a lower level of the canyon and the searchers had to climb down to get to it. Two volunteers stripped down to their underwear and went into the pool to search more carefully. The pool was quite large—about twenty feet long and seven or eight feet wide in most places—and was between three and eight feet deep. It was very ample for swimming and the volunteers had to dive completely under water to reach several areas of the pool which extended under the surrounding boulders. Though the water formed a still pool, it was nevertheless sweet and good for drinking.

Undoubtedly Jim went swimming there and then left his undershorts in the water because they were partly made of elastic and floated, thus being the only item of clothing he had which would have stayed on top of the water as a signal. They also would have been visible from the air as they floated on the dark green water. And moreover, they were inessential, whereas his other articles of clothing were not.

Jim would, I'm sure, have stayed in the pool long enough to get genuinely refreshed. I can't imagine his having done otherwise, as he would have been as exhausted and dehydrated as I was, if not more so. Scott reported the bed of the canyon to be much cooler than the cliffs and hills above because the boulders gave a great deal of shade and the air and rocks did not have an opportunity to absorb as much heat. The sun shone directly into the depths of the canyon for only brief periods of time each day. So at least Jim would have been refreshed, though undoubtedly still weak, when he left the pool.

The volunteers spent forty-five minutes searching the pool. Most of the group had waited on the higher level during this time as it was still hoped that the dog would be able to pick up a scent in the canyon below. When it became obvious that the dog would not be coming, the searchers fanned out in the vicinity immediately surrounding the pool. Israel Schiller, one of the young volunteers, found a pair of sunglasses about twenty feet down the canyon from the pool. The wadi opened into two separate canyons just beyond the pool, and the sunglasses were found pointing to the left branch of the wadi. The group then divided into two, heading down both branches of the canyon.

Soon I heard someone calling me.

"Mrs. Pike, your brother wants to talk with you." The searchers were carrying walkie-talkie radios so they could stay in close communication with the command car. I ran to the jeep.

"Diane, we've found some sunglasses," Scott said.

"Yes," I said eagerly.

"They are black."

"Yes, they are mine," I answered.

"They look like a man's sunglasses."

Then the radio went out and I could not hear. "Please," I said to the lieutenant in charge. "Can't we go up higher where we can hear?" He nodded and started up the engine.

We drove to the top of the mountain, near the ridge of the canyon, but communication was not much better. I could hardly stand the frustration of not being able to hear or be heard clearly. I tried desperately to describe my sunglasses to Scott, saying they were very large and had a bar above the nosepiece—a separate bar connecting the two lenses. I couldn't tell if he understood or not.

At 9:40 the search party in the left branch of the wadi came upon a second pool. The men entered the water, and very shortly Scott was on the radio again. "Diane," he said, "we've found some contact lenses."

"Yes, they are mine," I said eagerly.

Scott went on, uninterrupted, "They are in a white plastic case."

"Yes, yes," I shouted impatiently. I had put an extra pair of contacts in my cosmetics case, which I had left with Jim.

"The cheap kind," Scott said.

"Yes," I insisted. "Those are mine. You must go on!" Then I could hear no more. I later learned the contact lens case had been found floating in the second pool, apparently left by Jim as a clue. Again, the case was white and floated: Jim had obviously hoped it would be seen. One of the men talked briefly over the radio in Hebrew and silence fell again. My restlessness was overwhelming, but within just a few minutes the radio came on once more.

It was Scott. "What kind of shoes was Jim wearing?"

"Loafers," I said.

"We have found his footprint," Scott explained. The volunteers had found the footprint and encircled it with rocks. Just beyond there, Scott found another. They knew they were Jim's footprints because there was a sharp heel mark, but a smooth sole. Had it been a Bedouin's footprint it would have been smooth with no heel, since they wear sandals; had it been a hiker or searcher it would have had tread marks.

There was more silence. I don't remember thinking or feeling. I simply waited, stunned. It seemed almost too much to absorb that after so long a time of waiting so many clues should be found at once.

"Get in the jeep in the shade," Shlomo called to me.

"I can't sit there," I started to protest. Then I remembered my promise and got in and sat down in the shade. It was about 10:30 in the morning.

Soon the radio came alive again. Shlomo listened intently and then began nodding his head. "They have found him," he said.

"Is he dead?" I asked.

"You already knew," he said, looking directly at me.

"He is dead," I said.

"You already knew," he repeated.

"Yes," I said slowly. "I knew."

We sat in silence a moment. Then little by little, as it came in on the radio, Shlomo explained that the body was in a very difficult place—on the side of a severe cliff. They could not get to it to get it off the ledge.

"Will the helicopter come?" I asked.

"I don't know," he responded.

I got out of the truck and wandered aimlessly around the jeep. I could hardly stand not to be able to do anything; the waiting was almost more than I could bear. Then I heard the lieutenant using the radio.

"Who is he calling?" I asked Shlomo.

"Major Givati," he said.

"Oh, please," I said desperately. "They mustn't tell the press."

"Why?" he asked.

"The family must not hear the news on the radio," I said. "Please ask Major Givati if he will call my family before he tells the press," I pleaded. "Please."

Shlomo passed on the message to the lieutenant. "What number should they call?" Shlomo asked. I gave my parents' number and name.

"It will be done," he assured me.

"Oh, thank you," I replied.

Again we waited. After some time, they told me Scott wanted to speak to me again. "Diane," Scott said, his voice sounding very strained, "we found Jim."

"Is he dead?" I asked, knowing the answer. "Scott, if he's dead, tell me."

The confirmation came. "Yes, he's dead."

## PEACE AND JOY

My head pounded in the sun. I had known he was dead, but now the reality began washing over me in waves of sadness and relief mixed together, numbing me.

"Do you want me to stay with Jim or shall I come back?" Scott was asking me.

My mind whirled. After days of searching, at last we had found Jim. "Stay," I urged. "Stay with Jim." Yet I knew Jim was no longer in his body. There was no reason Scott should wait down there. Yet to leave Jim alone again . . . no—it wasn't Jim.

"Come on up, Scott," I said, suddenly feeling very weary. "You might as well come up." I felt an unfair burden had been put on Scott to go through all of this. But I was so grateful to have him with me. I couldn't imagine what I would have done without him. And we might not have found Jim's body at all.

"They want to take you and your brother directly back," Shlomo told me. He had apparently been listening to conversations over the radio.

"No," I said. "I will wait here till they get the body. I want to go back with the body."

"Why?" he asked with a penetrating look. "Why?"

I shook my head, unable to explain. "I just want to go with the body," I said, knowing with my mind that I was making no sense, yet feeling unable to leave now that we had—after what seemed the whole of eternity—finally found Jim. "I just can't go without the body," I said weakly.

"But why?" Shlomo persisted. Then more directly, "You don't really want to ride with the body."

Again my reason told me he was right, and with my spirit I knew Jim was not there—and that he was OK. I lapsed into silence for inability to decide.

The men began to pass around sandwiches and fruit. I ate, feeling hungry for the first time in a long time. I tried to save some of everything for Scott so he could eat when he got back up from the canyon. Everything tasted good to me for the first time since Monday.

Nearly an hour later, Scott emerged over the rim of the canyon carrying a big knapsack on his back. I put my arms around him in a clinging embrace. We both wept and laughed at the same time. "I'm so glad we found him, so glad," I said through my tears.

"I know," Scott replied. Then he pulled away. "I hope they understand why we're so happy," Scott said.

"I'm sure they do," I nodded.

Scott turned then, putting down the heavy knapsack he was carrying. Drinking from the water offered to him by the men, he said, "My friend is sick."

"What do you mean?" I asked.

"He's sick to his stomach. At first he was worried about me. He wouldn't let me carry his knapsack or anything. Then finally he couldn't go on at all, so I carried the knapsack. He needs lots of water. He had no water the last half hour. If he hadn't come with me they would have made me stay in the wadi."

Later Scott explained that when we embraced he had felt as though he would be suffocated. I understood that. I remembered back to that night when Jim had laid his left arm over me and I had asked him to move it because the weight was too much. In the desert each man has all he can do to cope with his own body. He cannot—because of the physical drain of strength caused by the extreme heat and the almost complete lack of any moisture in the air—stand over any length of time the added drain of energy which physical contact with another causes. And that regardless of the great pleasure physical contact under ordinary circumstances might bring, as had been the case with Jim and me.

I offered Scott some fruit and asked Shlomo if there were any sandwiches left. He said of course, and I suggested that Scott get some. After Scott finished eating, the officers again said they wanted to take Scott and me back immediately. Did we want to go to Bethlehem or back to our Jerusalem hotel? I checked with Scott to be sure and then said, "Please take us to our hotel."

They explained again that it could be hours before they would be able to remove the body. The helicopter found it impossible to reach the place where Jim had fallen, but no one could climb up or down to it either. When they were finally able to remove the body, they explained, they would take it by ambulance to Tel Aviv and the Institute of Forensic Medicine, where the autopsy would be performed. I would be required to go to Tel Aviv early in the morning to identify the body.

I acceded to all that they said now. I was suddenly very weary and knew there was no point in my staying there to ride into town with the body. Scott had indicated he did not want me to see it.

"It looked so pathetic," he said, his voice choking. "So unworthy of Jim. When I first saw it I ran forward and shouted, 'Jim, it's Scott and Diane! We're here! Jim, it's Scott and Diane! We've come!' The tears streamed down my face. There was no response at all—no movement.

"Then I borrowed some binoculars and looked more closely, since we were clear across the canyon from where he was. His left arm was completely black, as though charred by the sun. It made me sick to my stomach to see it, Diane. I don't want you to see it."

I was not convinced—I did want to see the body. Somehow for my own satisfaction that it was indeed Jim's body—after all those eternal days of searching—I needed to see it. But I did not have to see it out here. It was not necessary that I accompany the body back to Bethlehem. I knew that. Jim would somehow know I had been here till we found his body. He would know. And my accompanying the body back to town would not make the knowledge any more certain.

Within a few minutes we were on our way toward the Dead Sea. The two officers who had been with the search party all week sat in the front. I sat in the back of the jeep with Shlomo, Scott and an Israeli soldier who spoke no English.

We rode in silence most of the way down the steep, switchback road to the Dead Sea. Toward the bottom of the road, Shlomo, who had his transistor radio held tightly to his ear, nodded his head. "It is in the news now," he said.

"About finding Jim's body?" I asked.

Shlomo nodded. "Yes, they have it all now."

I felt nothing. I was glad to know that the family had had the news first. I had no conception of what it would mean for the rest of the world to know that he had been found.

I felt a great sense of relief to know what had happened—that he was in fact dead. To have gone home without knowing would have been torturous. I would always have wondered: "What if we had searched longer, farther? Could he have been found? Was he still alive? Had we done all we could?" For me the reality of his death was far easier to accept than not knowing would have been. For now, that knowledge was sufficient.

I suppose somewhere deep inside me I had known from the beginning—sometime around noon on Tuesday—that Jim was dead. And while I kept hoping that we would find him and that somehow he would be alive, I was also trying to prepare myself for his death. I had begun to write a statement for the press about it and to make notes about things to do regarding a burial and a memorial service. I had had the notes nearly completed by Thursday when Scott arrived. He had read the statement then, but I showed it to him again now. All I had added were expressions of thanks to all who had been so helpful to me during that long week.

"Is it OK?" I asked after Scott had read it. He nodded slowly, sadly. "Yeah," was all he said.

The long ride to Jerusalem passed with small talk. We learned of Shlomo's plans to study television and film production. He told Scott that the police had told him Scott was really great on the search. He said Scott ought to stay in Israel—that he ought to live there. Scott nodded, saying he would like that. "I've thought about studying at Hebrew University," he commented.

"You really belong here," Shlomo said.

I felt a great sense of pride in that. It was a genuine compliment to Scott, not only for his strength and courage through those days of search, but also for the sensitivity with which he related to the Israelis, genuinely appreciating them as persons and respecting their knowledge of the land and their integrity through the search.

Such responsive sensitivity to other men in their own culture and native environment is perhaps the greatest sign of love of one's fellow man that can be shown. Deep appreciation of those of other nationalities and ethnic groups as persons, and respect for their way of life *as theirs*, is a courtesy not always extended by Americans to foreigners or even to minorities in their midst. I was very proud of my brother, who at twenty had learned and manifested a lesson never mastered by many Americans even though they have had the same basic opportunities for education and travel.

Scott and I both said we were sure we'd be back to Israel. We felt a strange tie to and a warm affection for both the people and the land. We would be back—soon.

As we arrived back at the hotel it was shortly after 3 P.M. Two newsmen were waiting in the lobby, as were the assistant manager and several other hotel employees. They all greeted me with looks of compassion—a compassion which did not intrude or assert itself, but waited quietly to be drawn on if I needed it. I warmed immediately to their presence, greeting them and thanking them. They knew that my gratitude was for their understanding and support and they only acknowledged it with quiet nods. As I greeted individuals, each of them would say, "I am so sorry, madam." Tears filled the eyes of the Arabs. They knew, understood and shared my grief.

"I would be glad to have a press conference at 4 P.M.," I said to Mr. Petfalski, "if a room could be arranged. But I need to go to my room first."

"Of course," they all nodded. "At four o'clock."

Scott and I went to our room to call home. Mother answered again—and my brother Jim. I briefly told them about the search, my vision during the night which had given us such a tremendous sense of peace and joy about Jim's death, and the place the body was found. Then I said I wanted her, or someone, to talk with Jim's children and his mother about the burial.

"It seems right to me to leave the body here," I said. "I think Jim would want it that way. It seems to belong here." I couldn't express the depth out of which that feeling came; I couldn't imagine taking the body home. But I felt the family should be in agreement. They needed to share the decision.

"We'll talk with them," Mother assured me.

"We'll call back later," I said. "We're going now to a press conference."

There were only a few reporters there at four. Scott told about the day's search and I read my statement. Some reporters came in late. I answered a few questions, but then asked Mr. Steckoll of the Jerusalem *Post* if he would be willing to get my statement copied off for me so all the members of the press could have it. I didn't have the strength to go over it all again, I felt. He promised to do that.

When the press conference ended, Scott and I returned to our room. Peggy Barnhart of the consulate joined us and I asked her if she would inquire about burial practices and possible burial sites. She said she would be glad to. I asked about cremation and she said she thought it was against Jewish law, but she would see. She also knew there weren't many Christian burial sites and even fewer for non-Catholics. She promised to look into it all.

It hadn't occurred to me that there would be any problem about leaving Jim's body there. My first thought had been that we would scatter the ashes of his body over the Sea of Galilee. It was so peaceful and beautiful there and Jim loved it a great deal. If there could be no cremation, however, then burial in some appropriate place without embalming, so the natural processes by which the body returns to the earth could go on, would be fine. But it seemed impossible to think of taking the body home. It would put undue emphasis on that which was no longer Jim—a home he no longer inhabited.

Around 5 P.M. Scott got a call from Chief A Ben Schmauel and I got one from the sergeant who had dropped me off at the hotel. Both had the same message: the body was in Bethlehem. They wanted to go ahead with the whole process that night so they could get it over with. Special arrangements had been made at the Forensic Institute in Tel Aviv and the doctor was prepared to perform the autopsy that night. A member of the family was needed at once to identify the body.

"I will go," I said immediately.

"We will come for you at once. We will be there in ten minutes. And please," the chief of police said, "no press."

"We will be ready."

Within fifteen minutes the sergeant was there to pick us up. We had gone down a few minutes early to leave a note for John and Ellen Downing, who were arriving that afternoon from Santa Barbara. John is an Episcopal priest and the vice-president of the Foundation for Religious Transition—of which Jim was president—as well as the director of the Professional Refocus Operation (PRO), which the Foundation sponsors. Both had been started in the spring of 1969 to help in the personal readjustment of clergy and lay people who are disenchanted with the institutional church and find themselves in some kind of transition, whether with regard to belief, vocation and/or life-style. John and Ellen had worked very closely with Jim and me for six months and we felt them to be very special friends.

I had asked Peggy to arrange for someone to meet

John and Ellen at the airport, but we didn't know exactly when they would arrive. I felt sure it would be while we were gone, however, and so I left them a note:

> Intercontinental Hotel
> Jerusalem, Israel
> 5 P.M., Sept. 7, '69
>
> John and Ellen—
>
> Thank you for coming. We're sorry not to be here when you arrive. We have gone to Tel Aviv with the police to identify Jim's body. If you have not heard the details of today's search, the assistant manager will be happy to tell you all about it.
>
> Scott and I are both fine. Jim woke me during the night last night to let me know of his death. I'll tell you more. But we are at peace and *very* glad to have found Jim's body so we know what happened.
>
> See you shortly—
>
> Love,
>
> Diane & Scott

Then I asked Mr. Petfalski if he would be good enough to explain to the Downings what had happened if they did not already know. He nodded compassionately.

The sergeant drove us to Bethlehem. He told us we were very fortunate to find Jim, explaining that many times men get lost in the desert and are never found. No one had even suggested such a thing to us during the week. We were grateful indeed.

We were taken inside the police station, where they turned over to me Jim's traveler's checks, his glasses and my cosmetics case, all of which had been found with the body. Also on his body had been found his wallet with money in it, his watch and his ring, they explained. They did not find his passport or my camera, but everything else I had told them he had had with him was found. Nothing else was missing. They asked me to sign a receipt for the things I was taking with me.

"May I have the other personal effects?" I asked.

"Yes, of course. After the autopsy they will give them to you," the sergeant explained.

Then Chief A Ben Schmauel came to take us to the army headquarters, where the ambulance had taken the body. As we pulled into the yard, several dozen young soldiers poured out of their barracks and surrounded the jeep. There were already many standing around the box in which I knew Jim's body must be lying.

I started to get out of the jeep. An officer yelled something at the young men and they all went back inside.

"I want to explain very carefully what you will see before we go," the chief said. "You must be very strong, for what you will see will be very hard." He was looking directly at me.

"I am all right," I said, "I will be all right." I felt calm inside. I knew I would not be sickened at the sight of Jim's body.

"The desert is very hard on a man's body," the chief began. "Your husband is fortunate not to have died of the heat alone. He is very fortunate to have fallen, for to die a desert death is terribly painful and slow. The sun does terrible things to the body: After only six hours lying in the sun, a man's body turns red; in eight hours it turns blue and after twelve hours it is entirely black.

As the body dries out, it swells to almost twice its normal size. For this reason it is difficult to recognize a man who has been out in the desert heat more than twenty-four hours."

I was listening carefully, but I could not envision what the chief was trying to tell me. I tried to hear the words carefully—to listen intently.

"Now there is more you should know about your husband. He must have been dead at least four days; the body is extremely decayed. It is swollen, as I have said, to almost twice its normal size, but it is also decayed. The skin has turned black and the smell is very strong."

The story of Lazarus flashed into my mind: "Lord, by this time there will be an odor, for he has been dead four days." [John 11:39]

"You will have to be very strong," the chief was saying. "This will be very hard."

"I will be all right," I said again. I felt strong inside. I knew Jim was at peace.

"I wanted you to know exactly what you would see," the chief explained.

"You are very kind," I said. "I had no idea." I meant that. I had no idea. In the United States death is hidden from us. The bodies of our friends and relatives are preserved and transformed by plastic surgery to make them look as though they are alive when actually they are dead. We do not often see death in its harsh reality. It is ironical that we should want to have our bodies carry the *appearance* of life even unto death. We hide from ourselves in death (as in life) that our personhood does *not* originate in and terminate with the physical body which houses us for the brief period we spend here on earth. It is as though even in death we would worship the flesh. Yet we hate it too. We reject that which we worship. We are not free to love our bodies—yet neither can we let them go.

I loved Jim's body intensely while he was in it. I love my own body—then and now. But I was ready to see Jim's body in a state of decay, for I knew he was no longer at home in it—he had taken up residence elsewhere and nowhere. He was free now to be a true nomadic spirit, for "The wind blows where it wills; you hear the sound of it, but you do not know where it comes from or where it is going. So with everyone who is born from spirit." [John 3:8] Jim was no longer bound by this body. We got out of the jeep and walked toward the ambulance.

The body was covered with a light blue sheet and had been placed in a coffin-shaped tin box. As A Ben Schmauel led me up to the box, he lifted the sheet and began to pull it down, exposing the head. The stench was terrible and I looked to see Jim's head completely black and very enlarged. His head was turned to the left side so that I saw clearly only the right side of it, but I could see that his eyes were completely gone—there were only sockets surrounded by swollen flesh. His mouth was open, but his nose and ear were hardly distinguishable. His neck was so swollen that from the back of his head down to his back there was only straight black flesh—puffy. I could make out no hair on the head.

His shirt was pulled open in front, exposing a bare and very swollen chest. His right arm lay exposed, the sleeve pulling tight around the upper arm, the skin black and puffy. I pulled the sheet back to expose the remainder of his body.

The right leg was bent and caught up above the left leg, which was underneath. His pants were torn in the seat, exposing torn, raw flesh—red and white through the black pants and flesh. He still had his shoes and socks on, but his legs were also puffed, filling the stockings and bulging out of the shoes. His pants were pulled up, exposing more of the black skin.

As I looked Chief Schmauel said, "Is it your husband's body?"

I said, "Yes, it is my husband's body. It is his head, it is his shirt, those are his pants, his shoes and socks. Yes, it is my husband's body."

Then I added, "He had a watch and ring on his left hand." The left arm was under the body, so Chief Schmauel took the sheet and lifted it by the upper arm. As he pulled it out, it appeared limp. The watch was there, on a very black arm, as was the ring—the fingers were already eaten away by maggots, leaving red and white flesh exposed and the ring sunken in flesh and surrounded and covered by the larvae.

"Yes, they are my husband's watch and ring," I said. "I would like to have the ring."

"They will give it to you after it has been disinfected," he answered. Then he turned me around to lead me away.

As I turned, I found Scott standing right beside me. I put my arm around him and he his around me. "Are you OK?" he asked.

"Yes, I'm fine," I said, still feeling calm inside. "What about you? I thought you weren't going to look."

"I decided my imagination would be far worse than actually seeing," he replied, "and we have come all this way together. I wanted to be with you." I gave him another squeeze and we got in the jeep.

"For the first time I think I understand the immortal spirit," Scott said. "When you see the flesh like that you know there is no life in it."

I knew what he meant. As I looked at that black, swollen, maggot-eaten body, I could recognize that it had been Jim's, but Jim was obviously no longer in it—it was so obviously not Jim any longer that it seemed very right to me that the body should decay and return to the earth. It seemed to belong to the earth—to those rocks and that clay which had given support to my body as I climbed and which had given way under Jim's, only to catch it again on a tiny ledge as it plunged to the bottom of the canyon. His body now belonged to that ground and those rocks—mine was still inhabited by a life-giving spirit.

I realized that our burial practices in the United States deprive us both of the harsh reality and of the strange beauty of death. The reality of the mortality of the body —its fragile nature, succumbing in but a few hours to the elements when overly exposed—and the beauty of nature's way of using all things for the good of ongoing life in the cosmic sense, wasting not even a few hours before the process of transformation begins. From ashes to ashes and dust to dust: the body returns to the earth to be transmuted into life-giving matter once more. The web of life is strengthened even by death.

And as for the real Jim—Jim's spirit, the person—I had no doubt he lived on. I sensed no "deadness" in him. I felt no breach in our union—no severing of relationship. Before we took our marriage vows we made clear to each other that though we would say "till death us do part," we both knew not even death itself could separate us.

That affirmation overwhelmed me now as I sensed the freedom which the reality of having seen the dead body already in a state of decay brought. Never could there be any illusion about his death: the body clearly no longer had Jim's life in it. I felt great joy in the inner assurance I had that Jim had found freedom and fulfillment in his hours alone there in the desert—and in the hours after his death as he grew accustomed to the idea of leaving his body and became aware of those who were waiting to receive him on the other side. And there was a marvelous feeling of victory in the knowledge that death does not conquer the Life Force which flows in and through us, but claims only the time-and-space-bound flesh, freeing the spirit for new life and joy.

We returned to the police station and Chief Schmauel explained that at seven o'clock there would be a press conference so we could finish everything at once. He sat across a small table from us, with Scott at his side. He wrote on a small piece of paper, "Be strong. One hour." Then he said softly, kindly, "You must be strong. Tears are all right, but not here. When you are alone. But if, when you get in there, you cannot go on, I will step in. Be strong."

As we walked into Major Givati's office at 7 P.M. the floodlights were turned on. I sat to the major's right and motioned to Scott to sit at my right. Chief Schmauel was standing at Scott's right by the large display map. To the left of the major was an interpreter who announced to the press that first Major Givati would make a statement in Hebrew, which he would translate into English. Then Mrs. Pike would make a statement. Finally, he assured the press that any of us would be glad to answer questions. The conference proceeded as announced, and shortly after 8 P.M. A Ben Schmauel drove Scott and me back to the hotel in Jerusalem.

I told Scott to run ahead and ask the Downings, if they were in the lobby, to meet me in the room, as I was sure I would break down and I didn't want to greet them in public. He ran ahead. Then A Ben told me he wanted to walk with me to my room. He took my right arm as we walked along, and with his own special kind of compassion he said:

"There are three things I would like to say to you. The first is that I am only sorry that my English is so poor that I cannot tell you what I really feel in here (touching his chest). All I know to say is that I will never forget you or your husband.

"Second, there will be many people to carry on, but only the wife can really carry on. You must be strong.

"Third, you must turn now to the future. It is all right to having loving memories, but you must not look back. You must look to the future."

I tried to express again my gratitude, which he would not receive as due him, and he turned to go.

"We will be back," I said. "Until then—shalom." A Ben Schmauel, chief of the Bethlehem police, had been my pastor for one lifelong week. His pastoral care had been more direct, honest and unsentimentally loving than I ever remember experiencing. I felt extremely close to him—and admirative of his strength, his kindness and his ability to face the truth—reality—no matter how hard it might be.

Scott came down the hall to say the Downings were in a room two doors down. He went to get them. As they entered my room, we all broke into sobs. Tears flowed freely as we embraced for a long, long time. Then I began to fill them in on the story. I told them of my vision and of my certainty that Jim was in peace and joy. They received it all and then said they had many things to share in the morning. It was then 11 P.M. and we had to be up at 5:30 A.M. in order to be in Tel Aviv by seven for the autopsy report. Before going to bed I needed to call home to clear with the family about leaving the body in Israel.

The next day was an extremely long one. At the Forensic Institute a doctor gave us the results of the autopsy. He was not, unfortunately, the doctor who had performed the examination, so he could not give us very specific information. He did say that there appeared to have been no violence of any kind done to the body, that they found the circulatory system in good condition, that the ribs were fractured and that the state of decay of the body seemed to indicate Jim had been dead four or five days. He then handed me a burial certificate which said: Date of death: "(?) September 2, 1969"; Description of body: "Advanced putrefaction, fractured ribs." The cause of death was listed as "injuries from fall, exhaustion and exposure."

They asked me what my plans for burial were. I said his family had agreed with me that his body should be left in Israel. We were going now to find a spot and would notify them as soon as we had located one.

The doctor then turned over to me Jim's personal effects. I dug into one of the little bags and pulled out Jim's wedding ring, which I promptly pushed on with my own. We had selected their design because we felt they represented the open nature of life, the unexpected elements —grace—which come to us as gifts to be received and responded to in love. This completely unexpected turn of events in both our lives seemed appropriately symbolized by a union of our rings on one finger as I went on without Jim—yet united with him.

A quick trip to the American embassy to consult about funeral practices put us in contact with the Anglican priest at Immanuel Church in Jaffa, the Reverend Mr. Henry Knight. He received us warmly, as did his wife, and took us out to St. Peter's Cemetery, the only burial ground in the area for Protestants. He opened the gates to the walled-in grounds and we stepped into a quiet, shaded area. The Mediterranean Sea was spread out directly in front of us. We could hear the waves and smell the sea in the breeze.

On the level closest to the sea there was a lovely site available, shaded by a cedar tree. "That is just right," I said. "Just right. How soon can the grave be made ready?"

"By tomorrow morning, surely," the priest responded.

"Oh, please," I said, "couldn't it be done by this afternoon? I'd like so much to get it all finished today."

Soon it was arranged with the gravedigger, the Forensic Institute and the embassy. The committal service was set for 5 P.M., Israel time.

The Knights invited us for lunch following a quick shopping tour which enabled me to buy a blue and white dress (Israeli national colors) for the service. After a brief rest, a shower and a cup of tea, John Downing and I planned the service. It would be joy-filled—carrying the note of victory and thanksgiving which seemed so appropriate.

And so it was. We covered the box with a woven rug—a soft, warm gold color, a favorite of Jim's. As a parting, symbolic gesture, I placed a peace cross on the box ("I've put my pectoral cross away and I'll wear this simple brass peace cross till the American invasion in Vietnam is over," he had told thousands all over the U.S.A.).

"Peace and joy, Jim," I whispered to Jim—not to the body. "Peace and joy."

# MONOTHEISTIC MARRIAGE

"We'll write a book about our life together and call it Monotheistic Marriage." It was nearly 4 A.M. in Jerusalem, Sunday morning, August 31. We had just spent nearly four hours going over in detail our memories of our relationship—almost a liturgical rehearsal and celebration of our union, as I look back on it.

We lay in bed, curled up as one, flesh pressed against flesh, as we always slept. The joy which filled us was heightened by our memories. Everything was so perfect —almost too good to be true.

Only three years and two months had passed since I first met this "controversial" figure—the man at my side so full of love and warmth, tenderness and deep caring. When with him and communing physically, as we were then, or spiritually (we often shared more than words could speak by looking deep into one another's eyes and simply dwelling there), it was difficult to think of him as controversial. He was irresistibly lovable, soft, endearing.

Yet I knew and shared as deeply—and loved as fervently—that other dimension of him too: his ever questioning mind and his ability to boldly formulate ideas about and positions on issues in a way that left almost no one feeling comfortable. My mind would race to follow his as the ideas tumbled out, one on top of the other. He had to talk to sort them out: the logjam of insights and thoughts were allowed into the flow of conversation only after being organized and categorized and set forth in order. Additional information was always welcomed and suggestions as to the categorization were carefully considered. Then he would assign priorities to the various possible positions in relation to the matter being considered and take his stand.

Though always ready to re-evaluate, Jim knew where he stood on nearly every issue. He had an incredible tenacity—an unmatchable ability to argue his opinion or point. Yet his willingness to admit readily any error he had made or to change his mind when presented with new facts and information made it almost impossible for even his enemies to dislike him—or to discount him.

I had enrolled in two summer session courses, one on "The New Theology" and the other on "The New Morality," at Pacific School of Religion in Berkeley with Bishop Pike as teacher in June of 1966. I knew nothing of the man except that he had taken many bold stands, speaking out against what he saw as evils in the society around him, and I recalled having read of his son's death and of feeling for him, as I have felt for other public figures in the past, a sense of compassion—not only for the loss of his son in such a tragic way, but also because we, the public, knew all about it. I knew many harsh thoughts and criticisms would have been hurled his way, and probably unjustly, for none of us knew the inside story which could be the sole basis for such judgments, if they were to be made. It was my conviction that few of us—even in our own lives—feel we are in a position to judge once we know the full circumstances surrounding a tragedy in any man's life.

And finally, I had read that he had only recently returned from Cambridge, England, where he had pursued further theological studies, and that he was considered to be on the forefront of the development of new approaches to ethics and theology. I felt sure his courses would be stimulating and I thought I might as well learn something while pursuing my primary goal.

My principal interest had been to make one final effort to find myself a man who was eligible, concerned about ultimate questions and committed to service in the Church. I had long been all three, and at twenty-eight was trying to decide whether to finally give up my hope that I could share in such depth with a man and marry someone whom I loved and with whom I was most compatible—but who was outside the Church.

My dilemma had always been that in spite of my inner dedication and conviction, I was attracted more to men unrelated to the Church than to what I began to call "ministerial types." And though I loved the Church in the deepest way, I was most impatient with her, finding the institution inflexible, all too slow to change, and lacking in compassion and true love and concern for individual persons. So much within me responded to the secular, where it seemed there were often more genuine acts of justice and love done than in churches, yet I considered myself a deeply spiritual person.

So as a last-ditch effort I enrolled in summer school at that Berkeley seminary. True to my past experience, however, I met many interesting persons but found no one both eligible and interesting in the classes.

I was intrigued by the professor, however. I found him quite conservative in theology and rather inconsistent in his approach to ethics, having (I felt) based an existentialist approach on an ontological (i.e., unchanging) value base of "right" and "wrong," "good" and "evil." But what was far more important than the particular views he held, as far as I was concerned, was that he was an excellent teacher. Having sat in many lecture halls during my five years of higher education, having taught four years myself and being responsible for teacher training and preparation for the church in which I was then employed, First United Methodist in Palo Alto, I knew something of the rarity of a "master" teacher. And seldom had I known one who had already earned his fame as a scholar, author or researcher in his field.

I admired Bishop Pike's ability to organize and present a lecture without notes and was intrigued and amused by his diversions into "side thoughts" since my best friends often kidded me about doing the same, registering their feelings of anxiety that I would never be able to work my way back to the main line of the story or thesis—then amazement and relief each time I finally did. Obviously Bishop Pike was a master at that "art," if such a style can thus be elevated.

But more than anything, I found him very open, receptive and responsive to questions, to criticisms and challenges, and to his students as persons. He had the gracefulness to receive an ill-informed question and answer it in such a way as to make the questioner seem helpful, significant and even essential to the day's discussion and to enable the class to benefit from new insights or illustrations in relation to every issue raised.

On the other end of the scale he was equally gracious: A just criticism was readily acknowledged as such and appreciation expressed; new information was relished and absorbed with a delight for having learned something new, and he usually requested the person write out the reference for him so he could "see for himself"; and questions to which he knew no answer were held up, examined and then tucked away with a "I'll have to think about that," or "I never thought about it just that way," or "I wish I could say I knew the answer to that, but I don't. Perhaps you'd be good enough to look it up for us all and inform us," or "I need to do my homework on that one. We'll take it up again next time." And the latter he never failed to do.

So I liked and respected the teacher and felt the three weeks of classes, meeting twice a week for six hours each day, would be profitable even if I didn't meet the man I was looking for. I entered into the classroom discussion in the ethics course by challenging hard at every point where I saw an inconsistency. I was joined by others—especially a UCC minister—in my attempt to make Bishop Pike see that a truly situational ethic precluded any set of *absolute* values, no matter how fundamental they seemed. He never yielded the point, but he did a lot of grappling with it.

At the same time, a second level of communication began between the professor and me. During the afternoon break on the first day, the Bishop asked if there was anyone going to San Francisco after the class. I raised my hand. He pointed my way and said, "Fine, I accept. I'm without a car and need a ride back to the Cathedral."

So it was that we met personally. I drove him back to San Francisco on that day and on four more of the six days of classes. On each occasion we had about forty-five minutes for private conversation. No personal words were spoken between us during those brief encounters, but a deep bond of communication was established unlike—or at least deeper and more intense than—anything I'd ever experienced before. As we talked, I would look across the car and our eyes would meet. There was a profound recognition: something extraordinarily deep.

I knew nothing about his personal life (except that he was married and was "too old" for me anyway), but in spite of all (and the lack of any personal exchange of words between us) I went home after the second ride across the bridge and said to my roommate: "Shirley, this is going to sound very strange, but when I am with Bishop Pike I feel as though we're already married. It's like, literally, a 'marriage made in heaven'—a full-blown relationship which has just been dropped down over us without our doing a thing to make it be."

In the weeks and months ahead—on scattered opportunities when we were together for a few hours at a time—we both experienced the fullness and richness of that observation of mine. There was no need to get acquainted: we already knew each other. Each of us would share "facts" from our past, which filled in a few details here and there, but we already knew in a deeper sense—there was nothing "unknown" to learn about each other.

Moreover, we got along so well it was as though we had had years to establish patterns of relating. Our tastes and decisions were remarkably similar and our styles of life amazingly complementary. Our points of view and attitudes were in almost perfect harmony, and as personalities, neither of us overwhelmed the other. It was all a joyous experience for us both.

I had never thought much about reincarnation before then, but the thought frequently passed through my mind that first year: "Could it be that we were married in a previous life?" The question goes unanswered, but the depth of our union doesn't make it seem an irrelevant or utterly ridiculous query. At the least I can affirm that right from the first meeting neither the sum total of hours spent together, nor the length of the span of time we'd known each other, nor our respective chronological ages seemed to have any correlation with or effect upon the depth of our relating. Our union was prior to any verbal or physical exchange of affection. As it was "made before time," we did not expect it to be altered by death.

These were some of the things we recalled that night in Jerusalem. We shared again our thoughts and feelings regarding each encounter and rejoiced in and offered thanks to God—the source of all grace—for the priceless gift which was ours. As we wondered at the beauty of our love—at the joy we found in each other—at our perfect union which made us one yet left us each perfectly free at the same time, we pointed to a particular conversation we had had in November of that first year as the key to it all.

I had shared on that occasion—the first time Jim had had an entire Saturday evening free since I'd met him—a "devil" I'd been wrestling with and had finally conquered: the temptation to put Jim at the center of my life, to let all meaning for me flow through and from him, to focus my thoughts on him, to wait in animated suspension between our meetings—in effect, to make him "god" of my life.

Jim's comprehension was complete. "The problem of idolatry," he said. "Of course, that would be a big mistake for either of us. But you could not do that any more than I could. 'Hear O Israel, the Lord thy God is *one* God and thou shalt have no other gods before Him!' That is the great commandment in the light of which all other ethical claims fall into their proper places. Neither of us could live any differently."

It was settled between us. We reflected on it many times but the reality never faltered. Our individual centers were made one in a common dedication of will and in a common act of faith in the One who is above, below, within, through, before and beyond all else— who is no thing and no person, but who is all and is certainly no less than personal—the One, the Ground of all Being, *The* Life, God. Ours was/is a monotheistic marriage—idolatry of even the beloved "other" had fallen by the wayside and we were free to be fully united in serving God, in quest of the Truth, together.

In the fall of 1967 the merger of our professional and personal lives began. I moved to Santa Barbara to act as executive director of the little corporation, New Focus Foundation, which coordinated all of Jim's speaking and writing commitments, assisting in both research and correspondence. This association enabled us to share nearly all of our professional interests and concerns. Jim's full-time post at the Center for the Study of Democratic Institutions contributed to what we shared, as both of us had deep concerns about the state of our society and the growing malaise of many of our democratic institutions.

On the personal side, Jim's wife, from whom he had been legally separated for over a year before I met him, filed for divorce in the summer of 1967. This left us free to begin going places together socially, thus building a community of friends in Santa Barbara and starting to make mutual friendships out of our past associations. The joy and unity we shared grew as our circle of relationships expanded. We began experiencing an axiom that both of us had long held to be true—but had never had the privilege of sharing with another: love multiplies, it doesn't divide.

Together we launched into two intensive projects related to our mutual search for truth. One had to do with the psi factor in the human personality—that dimension of the human personality or psyche which transcends time and space—and culminated in our co-authoring *The Other Side*. The other was Christian origins—a study Jim began a year before I met him, but which I now entered with him. Through it we hoped to discover the key for both of us to the deep faith we shared—which was rooted in our Christian heritage, certainly, but not limited by the dogmas or creeds of the Church—and to our common love for the Church, in spite of all her failings.

The two studies were not unrelated. The more we learned about the psi factor, which manifests itself in dreams, experiences of cosmic consciousness, prayer, extrasensory perception, precognition, retrocognition, powers of healing and exorcism, speaking in tongues and psychic phenomena, the more we became aware that it is this very dimension of man's experience which is at the core of every great religion. Certainly Christianity grew out of the profound conviction of a small group of men that Jesus had been—and continued to be—filled with the power of God. The principal evidences of this were the psi experiences they had with and through him: healings, exorcisms and most important, the resurrection—seeing and talking with him after his death.

Our excitement grew as we learned more and more about both fields. We hoped we could help contribute to the freeing of modern man to explore scientifically—with understanding and without fear—these realms so often bound up in superstition. The rediscovery of Jesus as a man and of the style of life which enabled him to stay free of false gods—idolatries—gave us new hope for a model for personhood in this era which would enable man to develop his full human potential. We saw this as hope for the Church too, if people still had ears to hear.

It is not too surprising, then, that when it was possible for us, because of the finalizing of Jim's divorce, to have our union solemnized and publicly blessed, we sought permission to be married in the Church. Our union was already centered in our faith and in our love for the Church, and certainly God had blessed us in it more fully than we had ever dreamed possible. We were eager to share that joy with our family and friends in the celebration of the Eucharist—an act of thanksgiving.

Though neither of us felt the Church—or a given man on behalf of the Church—should have the right to pass judgment on any relationship, yet we knew the canon law of the Episcopal Church, and until it could be changed we were willing to abide by it. So we applied to the Sixth Bishop of California, Jim's successor and old friend the Right Reverend C. Kilmer Myers, for a judgment which would declare Jim's past marriage spiritually dead, thus enabling us to be married by an Episcopal priest according to the laws of the Church. We also asked Bishop Myers if he would himself act as the marrying priest.

The latter request he granted us first, agreeing to marry us on November 14 at Grace Cathedral in a solemn High Nuptial Eucharist. All plans were laid, participants invited and families and friends notified of the occasion.

Then Bishop Myers, under pressures he has never fully revealed, reneged. He said he did not feel he could give his blessing to our union. He did, however, give us a formal judgment as to Jim's former marriage—declaring it spiritually dead in the eyes of the Church—which enabled us to be married by an Episcopal priest, though of course plans for the place for the wedding had to be changed.

The reversal of plans caused a delay and it was not until December 20, 1968, that we finally had that joyous celebration we had looked forward to—in my family church, Willow Glen United Methodist, in San Jose. Four clergy friends took part—Dr. Stephen H. Fritchman of Los Angeles, a Unitarian; the Reverend Ralph Fellersen of San Jose, a Methodist; the Reverend Hugh Anwyl of Los

Angeles, a Congregationalist; and the Reverend Robert E. Hoggard of Santa Monica, an Episcopalian. The service was according to the Episcopal Book of Common Prayer and was set in the context of a service of worship, with hymns and guitar-accompanied songs shared by the small congregation of family and friends. Father Hoggard solemnized the marriage and blessed us on behalf of the Church.

The occasion was appropriately joyous and filled with love. An incomprehensible blow followed three days later when Bishop Myers, apparently in a moment of anger, issued a personal request to all his clergy and to all the bishops of the Episcopal Church that Jim no longer be invited to perform any priestly function—preaching, ministering the Sacraments or holding any public service—in any Episcopal church in his diocese and, as far as his request would be honored, elsewhere throughout the country.

The effect was immediate and complete. Though Jim had in no way violated any law of the Church, though Bishop Myers did not state any offense on Jim's part, though as Bishop of California he had no such powers and though his request constituted an absolute violation of due process, amounting to deposition without charges, hearing or trial, no further invitations were extended to Jim from priests in the diocese of California and all Episcopal preaching engagements Jim had accepted in other parts of the country for the remainder of the year were canceled.

We were both stunned by the blow—as much by its effectiveness as by its injustice. None of those who tried to intercede on Jim's behalf with Bishop Myers could get him to rescind his request; a committee of bishops of the Episcopal Church, appointed by the Presiding Bishop to meet with Jim and Bishop Myers, made no suggestions as to a resolution of the conflict; and the Presiding Bishop himself never so much as wrote to, or talked to, Jim about the difficulty, even though Bishop Myers had publicly announced that he had turned the matter over to him.

After much soul-searching and heartsick reflection, Jim and I decided we had only two alternatives: we could ask for a trial to clear Jim's name, knowing there was no will to justice or to truth among the bishops when it came to matters which might cause "controversy" and that they would more likely than not find a way around canonical procedures; or we could leave the Church. If we did the former, we knew we would have to give a great deal of time and energy to an exercise which we felt would bring benefit to no one else—and possibly not even to us. If we did the latter, we could avoid Jim's carrying the title of "bishop," which was now a sham, since he was not allowed to function within the Church as such, but we could get on with the real work and ministry of a bishop: keeping the truth of the Church's message, teaching and pastoral care. We decided for the latter as the most productive in the long run—and as a more appropriate expression of our priorities and interests in any case.

But we were both deeply hurt. We decided to try to turn that pain into a creative thrust by forming a Foundation for Religious Transition, hoping to formalize our ministry to all those who, like ourselves, found themselves on the edge of institutional Christianity—whether inside or out—and who had deep religious concerns and needs which for many were going unmet. That was in April of 1969.

Our new Foundation was launched with enthusiasm and the response indicated it could indeed help to meet the needs of many. But Jim's hurt over having to sever his formal ties with the Church continued.

On our way to Israel in August, we spent several long hours—and into the early morning—in Paris one night trying to deal with that open wound: "Why does it hurt me so much," he kept asking, "when I know all that is wrong with the institution and also know that our leaving the institution does not cut us off from the tradition or in any way alter our ministry?"

"It is because of the lack of any caring on the part of so many of your bishop friends," I said. "Their lack of comprehension of your depth of love for what is the heart of it all—for the *raison d'être* of the institution—is what hurts. If we felt they understood, and cared as deeply, we would not mind so much leaving the tradition in their hands."

But we had no assurance of that except on the part of a limited few, and Jim walked to his death in further search of the Truth—with a wound unhealed about having been cut off by his brethren in the Episcopate.

Perhaps it can be understood, then, why I immediately began referring to my husband as Bishop Pike again—as soon as he was lost in the desert—and why I asked for a solemn High Requiem Mass for him in Grace Cathedral —which he had completed during his Episcopate in San Francisco and which he loved. His deposition had not yet been acted upon; he was still a bishop in good standing.

If it is less simple to comprehend my personal request that Bishop Myers be the chief celebrant at the Requiem Eucharist, it should be said that that was in the spirit of my husband, who—no matter how much he had been hurt or how much injustice had been done him—never held a personal grudge against any man. He knew no vengeful feelings, harbored no personal resentments. He loved—by his actions as well as his words—even those who behaved as though they were his enemies. He had no idolatries—not even that of self-preservation.

Jim was, in my opinion, a man of true faith, and it was that faith which lent such depth to our union—an unidolatrous, monotheistic marriage.

# A JOURNEY'S END

The roots of monotheism are found deep in the wilderness tradition. For generations, prophets of the religions of the book—Judaism, Christianity, Islam—have come out of the desert to protest the idolatries, the fixities, of their people. Over the centuries, men in these same traditions seeking to purify their intentions or to prepare themselves for the task they felt called to do have withdrawn to the wilderness to meditate and pray—to be in the presence of their God.

The desert strips away all false securities. In the barrenness of the wilderness, all other supports fall—even that of one's own intellect—and one is laid bare to the One God, The Power, the constant Source of all Life and the Root of all security.

Jim and I went out into the wilderness in order to get a direct feeling for that—to know firsthand what the prophets have spoken of for generations. The past year had more and more led us there. We had been living the life of urban nomads—consciously choosing not to put our trust in fixities, such as possessions, or in false idols, such as reputation, position or persons. At the same time we had tried to open ourselves more and more to the creative Life Force we knew surrounded us, and in relation to which alone could our full human potential be realized.

For Jim it had been a long journey. As a child he had

been raised a Roman Catholic. He was very devout in his religion during those early years—a daily communicant with a vocation to be a priest. But because he took it all so seriously, seeking to practice and to believe all he was taught, he found himself with problems of faith and authority as a college student at the University of Santa Clara. He had been taught that the Pope was infallible; he felt the Pope was wrong in his encyclical on birth control;[1] therefore, he felt the Pope could not be infallible.

There began Jim's quest for the Truth, which could not be limited to man's ability to comprehend or express it. He sought Truth in the big sense—all-encompassing Truth which would not have to leave outside its purview any fact about life as man experiences it. Any formulation of the Truth which had to leave out a facet of human experience or which contradicted the nature of any known experience would have to be rejected or altered.

Jim left the Roman Catholic Church. Having earned his doctorate in jurisprudence at Yale and having become a successful trial attorney in Washington, D.C., and law instructor at George Washington University, however, he began to search for deeper truth: there had to be something more than financial and professional success.

So he re-entered the Church through Episcopal doors and soon began preparing for the priesthood. Once again he ran headlong into success, moving rapidly from positions as a tutor at General Theological Seminary in New York, to rector of Christ Church, Poughkeepsie (New York), to chaplain of Columbia University and chairman of its Department of Religion, to Dean of the Cathedral of St. John the Divine (New York City), to Fifth Bishop

[1] The encyclical letter *Casti Connubii*, December 31, 1930.

of the Diocese of California. The rate of his advancement left him little time for reflection, but once he had become through his office as bishop a "guardian" of the faith, a pastor of other pastors (*pastor pastorum*) and a teacher of the faithful, he renewed his search. What he guarded, counseled and taught needed to be as close to the Truth as it was possible for him to know. He felt the Church had made false idols out of what he called the three C's: Creed, Code and Cult.

So it was that the 1960s saw James Albert Pike—always outspoken on questions of social justice, equal opportunity for minorities, censorship, etc.—plunge into a re-examination of not only his own theological premises, but those of the Church. He sought not so much to bolster the tenets of faith as they had been passed on for generations as to look anew at the way things are and then to evaluate the Church's verbal formulations of Truth in the light of reality as a twentieth-century man knows it. Plausibility in the light of the facts was to become his major test for beliefs.

That search for theological truth—for more adequate conceptual formulations of the nature of reality and of man's relationship to it—brought Jim eventually to a study of the origins of Christianity. Verbal constructs should not get in the way of our making an act of will to trust—or place our faith in—the One who is the Ground of All Being. Creeds should not be absolutized.

Logical corollaries were Code and Cult. The mores of man—those rules by which social man controls his conduct—are also relative: they are formed and altered to meet the needs of the age in which he lives. There has been no "unchanging moral law" even in the history of the Christian Church. Nor should there have been. There is, Jim reminded those who would listen, only *one* moral claim, and out of it stems all others: You shall love the Lord your God with all your heart, and with all your soul, and with all your mind, and with all your strength. (cf. Deut. 6:5, Matt. 22:37, Mark 12:30 and Luke 10:27) No code of law can substitute for man's responsibility to this moral claim of God upon his life.

As for cult, only God is to be worshiped. The temples built in his name and the orders of worship or the particular modes by which we offer that worship should not be elevated above God himself. To do so is indeed idolatry. God does not dwell in temples made by hands nor is he pleased by our sacrifices before him, prophets through the ages have made clear. The only true worship is the offering of a man's life in faith—the act of will which says "I will go forth even if I do not know where I am to go,[2] for God is there before me and He will be the source of grace sufficient for all my needs in each situation— needs for insight, understanding and strength."

Jim found the roots of the three C's in the desert tradition. All great prophets have come to their utter dependence on God through long periods of fasting, meditation and prayer in the wilderness. There they rediscovered the great commandment: "Hear O Israel, the Lord our God is *One*." And it was also in the desert that these men were filled with the Power of God—enabled to speak with authority—for they had known and experienced that One Reality of which they spoke.

This was true also of Jesus: "His divinity is in the fullness of his true humanity, his total readiness to be a man, that is, the full, active vehicle of God's meaning and love."[3] And that total readiness to remain open to God,

---

[2] Cf. Hebrews 11:8.

[3] James A. Pike, *A Time for Christian Candor*, New York: Harper & Row, 1964, p. 113.

Jesus was able to maintain, if we can trust the accounts we have in the New Testament, only by periodic withdrawals into the wilderness.

The statement quoted above goes on to assert that the same possibility is in all men. Jim was seeking to open himself more and more that the fullness of his humanity might be realized. He broke through the idolatry of reputation, deciding to "say it the way it is" regardless of the cost of "what people will think." He broke through the idolatry of institutional success, realizing that rising to the top in either the secular or the religious did not ensure that one touched base with the Ultimate—indeed, might even prevent it. He broke out of the idolatry of religion itself, recognizing that each man must rediscover and affirm by *his own act of will* that Truth to which the Church's teachings and worship have tried to point.

These breakthroughs led him to speak out boldly, not only on social issues, but on matters of belief and on the crisis of authority in the Church, leading to charges of heresy—though no trial was ever held—and to a formal censure by his brother bishops for irresponsibility and a vulgarization of the Faith. Eventually he resigned as Bishop of California, feeling that if he were free of the administrative responsibilities of a diocese he could better pursue the Truth, act as a pastor to clergy and prepare himself for and carry out the teaching ministry to which he, as a bishop, was committed.

Toward the end, he had come to believe that the institutional church was not adjusting fast enough to the needs of urban man for more relevant religious "vessels" ("But we have this treasure in earthen vessels, that the excellency of the power may be of God and not of us." II Cor. 4:7), and that some of us on the edge of that institutional life—those who were not "eating out of the trough," as Jim used to say—would have to make the breakthrough to new expressions of faith in our age. He saw the need for a religion for the new urban nomad.

That search took us into the wilderness, both figuratively and literally. Figuratively, we had announced we were leaving institutional religion, moving out—not knowing where we were to go—as persons of faith, trusting that God was there before us. Literally, we went to the very area where the prophets have found their inspiration in ages past.

Though the first process had just begun and had not had an opportunity to bear full fruit, the second was not disappointing. As I look back on the whole journey, we both seemed determined—almost driven—to get out to that seemingly desolate spot where, in the end, none of our ordinary human resources of mechanical power, physical strength or reasoning were adequate to the situation. There we were thrust into that very wilderness experience which the prophets knew so well: We were dependent on God, and God alone.

When that realization settled over us—when we knew death was as much a possibility as life—a great peace came over us both. We rested in our faith that God is on the other side of death too, and that even in death there will be grace sufficient for all our needs. We trusted—had faith—that God would provide.

It was our custom to do everything together; but the final journey through the wilderness needed to be a solitary one, it seems. It seems somehow fitting, though that was not at all my conscious intention when I left Jim, that we should have spent those last hours alone. When I set out by myself, it was in perfect peace and without any fear. The strength which flowed through me and the insights I gained were not of my doing—they were of that Power which surrounded and filled me. They were from God.

I feel certain Jim's experience was not unlike my own, though perhaps it was more profound. He went into the wilderness with a deeper appreciation of its significance than I. Somewhere in the depths of his being a chord had been struck by his research, and his thought about it, which was in harmony with the vibrations of that land and its history. He was open to the depth of meaning it held for him and since April had been telling me that he felt the big breakthrough—spiritually—would come for him on our trip to Israel. We planned it with that in mind, leaving plenty of time for just sitting and drinking it all in—time in the wilderness, time at Masada, time at the Sea of Galilee.

I have no doubt that that breakthrough came for Jim during his hours alone in the desert. It could not have been otherwise for him, and the confirmation for me came in that vision I received on Sunday morning just before we found his body.

I would like to reflect for a moment on that. I have had many deep religious experiences of the kind most scholars would call "mystical"—though they were not a result of, nor did they result in, a withdrawal from the world—but I had never before had a "vision." I knew other persons who had, however, and on many occasions Jim and I had studied and talked about the nature of such experiences.

It was our conviction that insight and understanding break through to persons in various ways. To some they come in verbal formulations (e.g., the Ten Commandments), to others in symbols (e.g., Einstein's theory of relativity), to others in picture symbols (e.g., Peter's vision on a rooftop in Jaffa). The essence of the experience, however, is at the meaning level and must therefore, no matter what its form, be interpreted in order to be understood.

Nevertheless, there is usually a rather direct relationship between the actual circumstances of a person's life (or work) and the form in which the insight comes—sometimes more direct than others. Thus Einstein's theory of relativity was a reordering of the elements of his study, research and experimentation into a new configuration of meaning. The Ten Commandments were a codification of the life-style of the Israelites. And in Peter's vision he was offered as edible those things he had been taught not to eat as part of the religious law of his day. The meaning of each of these insights has been expounded in thousands of volumes—and still their potential has not been exhausted.

In the case of my vision, it seems to me there were several factors at work. There was Jim's death, which actually took place several days before my vision; there was my own distress, anxiety and faith/hope/doubt about our finding Jim; and there was a long-standing belief in life after death, based on images about the nature of it which stem primarily from my understanding of the Bible but which have been somewhat influenced also by my study of literature in the psychic field.

It seems to me that my vision must be understood in the light of all three influences. First of all, Jim had in fact died. My vision actually reflected rather closely the circumstances in which we found his body. There were distortions, of course, but the "picture" was amazingly accurate for extrasensory perception. The following elements corresponded.

## A JOURNEY'S END

When Jim's body was found (and Scott took pictures which confirm this), the only way it could be seen was from across the canyon—the same "view" as I had in my vision. He did appear to be lying on his left side, since the rocks he was caught on sloped down, thus rolling his body slightly over to the left, though not as much so as in my vision. His head was to the left (as it was in my vision), very near a crevice which went directly up to the top of that portion of the canyon. He did have his shoes and pants on and his glasses were at least with him —sunglasses still clipped on—when he was found, if not on his head.

There was a large overhanging rock which—though it was not smooth—prevented his body from being seen from above. There were also overhanging rocks to the left— though again, not smooth—and the wall of the cliff, just to the left of the crevice, did jut out toward the opposite side of the canyon.

I had seen Jim lying on a rather sizable ledge, whereas in actuality he was caught on what looks like a group of rocks caught in the crevice because of a boulder stuck there—rocks that might well break away one day—rather than a secure ledge. But the basic perception of the body position and the rock overhanging the "ledge" was correct.

And last, he was deep down in the canyon. It was a long way to the top of just the portion he had fallen into— and a great deal farther still to the top of the canyon. At the level where he had walked, there was indeed a hill, as I saw in my vision—in fact, a very steep one. And moving down the canyon to the east toward the Dead Sea was impossible because of a severe cliff—also reflected in my vision.

Therefore, what I "saw" actually correlated rather directly to the reality of where Jim was. That I did not have the vision at the moment of his dying is, I feel quite sure, explained by the second set of factors working in me. I was extremely anxious for and about Jim and still hoping and praying we would find him alive. During the entire week's search there was little ground for belief that we actually would find him—dead or alive. Had I known he was dead, however, it would have made it very difficult to ask the police to persist in the search. Yet to have had to leave Israel without having found him would have been agonizing.

It was only after the discovery of his undershorts in a water pool very near where he fell to his death that I received the vision. I feel this can be accounted for by unconscious controls which filter perception, allowing us to "see," or acknowledge or recognize, only what we are psychologically able to handle. Thus I probably received the "data" for the vision at the time it actually happened, but was only able to perceive it, or see it, when we were within hours of finding Jim. At that time it served as a preparation for finding his body, the assurance of which must also have been perceived unconsciously, rather than as a destruction of my hopes or of my will to go on with the search.

Finally, as for the perception of the departure of Jim's spirit, it is my belief that this reflects reality also. But precisely because it *is* my belief, it does not prove that such is the case. In other words, I believed firmly in life after death and would have expected Jim's spirit to go on even though his body had died. Thus it is possible that upon perceiving, by extrasensory means, his dead body lying on the side of a cliff, my unconscious, informed by

## A JOURNEY'S END

my beliefs, created a spectacular departure of his spirit for my own comfort, much as dreams are unconscious dramatic creations.

Whether the departure of Jim's spirit and his reception by a host of others on the other side of death reflect reality or not, there is no question that my visualization of them was influenced by my previous experiences and convictions. Even during the experience itself I was aware of similarities in what I was seeing to things written about in the Bible, and I had also read literature about "spirit bodies." Thus my images could have born resemblance to those described by others because that is the way things are or because I had no other images to draw on.

Whatever the process, I am fully aware that the vision can "prove" nothing about Jim's death. I have pointed out the similarities between what I saw and what we actually found the next day by way of the position of Jim's body, the nature of the cliff, etc., only in order to indicate that the vision was not divorced from reality. That is the least which can be said, I think.

The most I would affirm is that the emotional content of the vision was also an accurate reflection: that the peace, the tremendous joy and the sense of elation at victory over the death of the body were actually Jim's feelings as he passed to the other side. But I am fully aware that I make a leap of faith so to affirm. I can in no way prove it—nor would I try. It is an affirmation of faith.

As for the visual images of his spiritual "body," the "cloud of witnesses," the ascension, the filmy column (in Ecclesiastes, in psychic circles and in most Eastern religions called the silver cord) which attached the spiritual body to the psychical body—these seem unessential to me. It does not, to me, matter one way or the other whether they reflect reality, though I have been interested since then to read reports of similar experiences described by others.

I have no doubt that we are more than our physical bodies—countless experiences have given me ample evidence of that, not the least this last one in the wilderness in Israel—but more than that I do not need to know now. I have often thought, during these past weeks, of the statement Jim made about life after death whenever he was trying to explain why it concerned him very little: "I'm a one-world-at-a-time kind of guy," he used to say. "I'm coping now, and when the time comes, I'll try to cope then." I find that a healthy—and not inappropriate—comment which reflects how I feel about "knowing" the nature of the spiritual body: there will be time enough to find out when the time comes.

I have written at length about my own experience—vision—because it has seemed more appropriate, knowing it better than any other, to analyze it in depth than anyone else's vision or message.

It is a fact, however, that while the search was on in Israel, I received numerous reports of messages and visions from persons all over the United States, Canada, England and Israel. The messages did not begin to reach me until Wednesday evening, more than forty-eight hours after I left Jim, both because of the great time difference and because I was not in my hotel during the days to receive calls. My family in San Jose, California, also began to receive numerous calls from all over the country—many relayed by friends—on Wednesday. They continued to come in for the remainder of the week.

Because the messages were so numerous, it would be impossible to analyze each one in detail. They do fall into categories, however.

Several were quite off base in terms of the reality of

things—the desert itself, where Jim had gone, what had happened to him, etc. For instance, many people had visions of a sandy desert, whereas actually the wilderness area where we were is dry clay and rock. Some had visions of Jim being picked up by Arabs or Bedouin, describing their flowing clothes, etc., a few implying foul play, others indicating he was being cared for. Actually, the nearest Bedouin were the ones who helped us with our car that first day, but there is no evidence they even approached the canyon where we were.

Several people mentioned trees and bushes near the place he was lying—or covering the cave in which he could be found. Though there were a few small trees in the base of the canyon, and though there were some thornbushes on the cliffs, there did not happen to be any trees or bushes near Jim's body. And last, several tried to indicate, from their visions, the direction and distances Jim had walked. These messages did not, for the most part, match the facts, though at times they came close.

I am not disturbed by the fact that many persons had visions which were not accurate. First of all, it should be remembered that the initial reasoning of the police and Army, who know that desert very well, was also inaccurate. They were certain it was impossible for us to have driven where we did without wrecking our car, that it was impossible for us to have walked where we did and that it was impossible for a man to go as far as Jim went at the base of the canyon without using ropes.

Yet I did not—and would not—distrust these men because their analysis was not precise from the beginning. They were making their judgments on the basis of what they knew about men and about the desert. They did not know Jim and me, and we did not know the desert. These two facts made accurate reasoning nearly impossible—not because of any inherent difficulty in the process itself, but because these men simply did not have all of the relevant data at hand. I would not conclude from that experience that reason can never be relied upon. The police and Army were willing to risk their own lives and to give hours of their time under the most difficult conditions to find Jim, using their best judgment. No more than that can be asked of any man, and it is not a "fault" to be finite and fallible when you are a human being.

It would be even more difficult for persons who did not know the area at all, and who often did not know Jim and me either, to receive accurate impressions by extrasensory perception. Therefore, it does not surprise me that elements of what one would "expect," such as sand and Arabs, as well as errors of direction and distance should have crept in.

But I do not therefore distrust *these* people for erring at the unconscious level any more than I do the Israelis for mistakes in the conscious reasoning process—nor would I reject extrasensory perception as useless or necessarily faulty. In both cases, the will and intent was to be as helpful as possible. That was all any of us could offer. My perceptions were in error and I was right on the scene! These acknowledgments only highlight the limits of our human nature—and I don't feel that is to be lamented, but only acknowledged, accepted and worked with.

There were many other messages which are impossible to evaluate because of the time span involved and because of the fact that Jim was walking through the canyon. Some of the messages about his being alive and in a cave could well have been true at various points in his journey through the wadi. That he was not in a cave when we found him does not prove or disprove anything. He could have been—undoubtedly was—at several points during those first ten to twenty-four hours.

Third, there were many visions or messages which caught the essence of the situation in which we found Jim, or at least had several of the essential elements right (as was the case in my own vision). These elements were:

1. *He has found shade.* In fact, the cliff he was lying on was in the shade most of each day.
2. *He is near water, or a well.* In fact, there were two pools of water within about two hundred feet of where Jim fell. He had been at each.
3. *The searchers have been close or are passing over him; opening not visible from surface.* The searchers had been nearby, and when they did finally get to the place Jim fell, they did pass over him and could not see him from above. It was only from across the canyon that his body could be seen.
4. *He is hurt, in a coma, unconscious.* The position of Jim's body was such as to indicate he did not move after falling (e.g., his left arm and his legs were caught under him in a most uncomfortable position). Had he been able to move (had he still been conscious), he surely would have.
5. *He is at the bottom of a crevice; in a dry narrow trench; there's a sheer drop; place unlikely to be explored because of drop; place where there isn't much space; up high; deep down.* All of these descriptions are accurate. He had fallen straight down about sixty feet below the level where he had been walking, and a hundred feet from

where he had climbed up, and was lying on a tiny ledge—or group of rocks caught in the crevice—still a long way from the bottom of the canyon.

6. *Signals may be possible; lenses.* Jim had left clues for the searchers, which were certainly "signals," and though most of us thought "lenses" referred to my camera, in fact two of the clues were glasses: one pair with a lens broken out of it and the other a pair of contact lenses in their case.

Though none of these impressions—including my own vision—were what led the searchers to Jim's body, it was when I told Major Givati about the specific directions we had received from visionaries that he honored his word and sent more searchers out, along with the volunteers. Therefore, indirectly the messages helped us find Jim—and they were directly related to reality.

One lady's vision was especially accurate. She is from Berkeley, California, and her vision came nearly three weeks before we got lost in the desert. It was precognitive—and the most complete and precise of any I have an account of. Her description of it is as follows:

> I saw two people, male and female—I did not recognize them—in a car somewhere out in a very deserted, barren, dry, hot region somewhere near the Dead Sea. I associated it in my mind with Ein Gedi [not far to the south of where we actually were] because my Hebrew tutor of some months ago had described that place to me at one point.
>
> I saw two people leave the car and then the female person dropped out of the picture entirely. I don't know what happened. Anyway, the male person went on for a while and I saw and felt him in a state

## A JOURNEY'S END

of exhaustion—absolutely dried out and very hot. And I saw him stumbling at that point, and gasping, and I felt the heat.

The area was very much like a dry wash, an area that was somewhat depressed, slightly eroded, full of somewhat smooth rocks like very large pebbles. [This is almost an exact description of the wadi we walked in as we left the car.]

But then—I don't know how far this was away from the dry wash—there was a cliff that was very, very straight up but, well, the rocks were somewhat rounded and had crevices in them so that there were very deep shadows in the rocks for hundreds of feet and then at the bottom of the rocks were even more shadows, because of fallen boulders and so forth. [This is a most accurate description of the cliff Jim's body was found on, including the large, smooth boulders at the bottom of the canyon below where he was caught on the cliff.]

And I had the impression that it might have been an area that had depressions, almost deep enough to be caves. [This is also accurate. What we called "caves" in the wadi were actually shallow areas ("depressions" is a good description) with overhanging rocks which gave some shelter from the sun. There were no caves in the usual sense of the word.]

This remarkably precise description was given to one of our secretaries on September 4, more than fifty-four hours before the body was found.

Nearly everyone—with only one or two exceptions, most notably Mrs. Twigg of London, who was mentioned earlier—felt Jim was still alive, though badly in need of help. It seems to me this confusion might be explained in part by the following three experiences. My vision brought with it a conviction that Jim's spirit had hovered near his body for at least three days. This is only an intuition, but it would mean that sensitives would have perceived him as still in or near his body and thus still alive.

My intuition matches what seemed to come through in a sitting with Mrs. Twigg on Thursday evening, September 4, at which Jim appeared to be in the process of making the transition (seemingly the same transition I saw in my vision on Sunday morning). In that séance,[4] Jim seemed to be saying that he was not afraid of death, but he wasn't anywhere. "I want to see you all. I can't see you. You would have thought they'd have opened my eyes a bit," he was quoted as saying, mentioning that there were a lot of people around but he couldn't see them.

And finally, a woman from Colorado had an experience which sums up many of my intuitive feelings about what happened, though she knows neither Jim nor me personally. She made this report to a mutual friend after the body had been found, but before any decision about the burial had been announced. I quote it verbatim, and without further comment, since of course there is no way any of it can be proved. I only report that it matches many of the feelings I have had.

> He had to die there. A recent religious experience became overpowering to him. He wanted to "go home."

[4] At the completion of this manuscript, I have not yet had an opportunity to hear the tape recording of that session. These comments, therefore, are based on fragmentary reports from Mrs. Twigg herself and from a press report about the séance in the *Psychic News,* London, September 13, 1969. An evaluation of the evidentiary nature of the session will have to be made at a later date.

## A JOURNEY'S END

He knew, at least subconsciously, that he would not return to this country on this last trip. Because of the controversy grown up around him he felt he could be of greater help on "the other side." He knew he was preparing his wife to carry on the work here. He shared everything of the work with her. He wanted her to know everything he knew.

She must carry on, especially with the book they were writing. It will be a great help, especially to church people. It will grow in importance, become almost a textbook. He would be very disappointed if she did not carry out "their" work. Even if she feels she is too tired, that it is too much for her to do, after a time there will be an increasing awareness for her of his strength and presence.

Why could we not reach his psyche—got the "blank" feeling? his son was protecting him from any interference until he had made a smooth transition. Mediums everywhere were trying to communicate with him and this was a detrimental "pull" which was being blocked off for his protection. Another thing, a very high Being—a "Christed One"—helped him make the transition and took his consciousness to a realm "higher" than mediums or we of this earth-realm could reach.

I wish that his wife could know that he did not suffer in dying. As it was reported that she said she had felt "out of her body" watching the falls and the hurts, without feeling them, so was he just watching what the body experienced. He was not "in" it, suffering what it suffered.

His work was finished as far as his doing it was concerned. That is why he chose his wife and prepared her to—what you would say, "be the instrument" for what he had planned—he had other things to do on other levels of consciousness. Oh, that Being (who came for him)—when I touched that level for a few seconds it was one of the highest I have ever touched. I wish those who knew Bishop Pike could have felt what I did—it was such a beautiful thing—they couldn't possibly want him limited to things "here" again. He was a much higher-developed individual than people knew. Even people who love him did not know what a developed Soul he was.

I got a flash of a previous time that he and his wife were together. They have been together many times —until they thought like one person instead of two. It went by so fast I could only guess the location, but he was a gray-haired man, she was a little girl, his daughter, about nine or ten. I would guess it was in biblical times because of the costumes, but they were very, very close—they wandered about. He was a dynamic teacher—something like a prophet—and they depended upon each other in a remarkable way. She went on doing what they did together after he died. That was all that I got on that.

His "time" being nearly up, the Reality in him knew that if he died in this country the attention on the "body"—the disturbance of it—embalming and all that; the focus would have been upon his *death*, holding his consciousness down, "earthbound." By being "lost" people's consciousness was focused more upon his *aliveness* and this permitted the necessary freedom for him to reach such a high state so quickly. It was very important that those who were close to him, especially his wife and close friends, keep hoping until he was "free" and strong enough to remain on that high level instead of being dragged down by their immediate grief.

It was a most beautifully "planned" transition as I saw it. I do so wish that his wife could accept or be made aware of the magnitude of the entire thing. She would be helped through her personal grief if she could see the whole picture.

I wish that she would let the body be left there—it would be his wish—he loved it so. It was "home" to him.

## *NO REGRETS*

The depth of my grief at the loss of Jim has grown, rather than lessened, during the weeks I have been back in the States. The intensity of his life, his unending energy, the vibrant electricity that filled the air when he entered the room are impossible to forget even in their absence. There is a vacuum which surrounds me in our home.

I miss everything about him: his marvelous sense of humor; his vital interest in anything new he could learn about any field of knowledge; his deep concern about and outrage at the injustices in our society; his love for and fascination with the Church—its tradition, heritage, decline, reform; his ability to see things whole, to get the big picture, to relate old ideas and get new insights.

And I feel the deprivation others have suffered at his loss. A bigger portion of every day was spent by Jim in personal counseling and pastoral care than in any other single activity—here in Santa Barbara or while traveling anywhere in the country. He cared deeply about persons and made himself available to them whenever they needed him—whether it was convenient in terms of his other obligations or not.

And of course I miss his expressions of love for me and my being able to reach out to touch him, caress him, kiss him. So many times each day we would say how much we loved each other or express it with a touch or a hug. Nearly every morning as he woke up (I nearly always awakened first) he would turn and look into my eyes and say, "How could I possibly be so lucky?"

We knew such joy with one another. I know it is only because of the depth of that joy—and the intensity of our love—that I grieve his loss so. And though I sense his presence daily—and know he is with me in a real way—it is not at all the same, and never will be again.

Yet I would not have Jim back. Not now. Not physically. Just as I feel we were both somehow driven by some inner force into that wilderness—seeking the experience, eagerly awaiting what it would bring us by way of insight, understanding and an experience of reality, of God's power—so I feel somehow this portion of Jim's odyssey was finished—his search for Truth at this time on this plane of existence somehow seemed to be completed.

There are so many little things that contribute to that conviction. As I look back over the weeks before we left for Israel, so much that we did points for me to some unconscious realization on Jim's part—or perhaps both our parts—that his journey in this phase was about to end.

He had left his job at the Center for the Study of Democratic Institutions at the end of June, so we had two full months, with very little travel, at home together all day every day. Of course, our home was always full of guests, but that added to the joy we shared together.

We spent one entire Sunday—at a time we could not afford to pause in our work—talking about his life in terms of his spiritual growth. He took me all the way back to his childhood to share each deep experience with me, interpreting its significance for me in terms of his growth toward personal—spiritual—freedom.

Just before we left, he withdrew his offer to waive his right regarding a hearing for his deposition, thereby ensuring that he would remain a bishop of the Church until after we had completed our trip to Israel and Europe.

We spent time with his children before we left for Israel, having to make a special trip to Sacramento and San Francisco to make it possible. Jim said he felt it was "important" we have time with them, and I felt, even at the time, that it had a deeper significance than any fulfillment of a "fatherly obligation" would have implied.

We spent a great deal of time with Jim's mother during the summer and he often spoke of feeling that our love had made it possible for his mother to be restored to him. For the first time in years, he reported, he looked forward to seeing her and thoroughly enjoyed the time spent with her. She, in turn, responded with a new life and love which are beautiful, still, to see. We took her with us the weekend before we left for Israel to my brother Jim's wedding, where she had an opportunity to get well acquainted with my family—so important to her feeling free to stay with them during that long week's search.

For the first time—in spite of all the traveling we did—we took out accident insurance on our lives before leaving.

Jim mentioned many times that he had never looked forward to a trip so much and that he knew a big breakthrough was coming in Israel.

When we arrived in Israel Jim said, "Dear, I didn't kiss the ground, but this is holy land, and I have come home."

Our second night in Jerusalem we stayed up nearly all night rejoicing in the detailed memories of our relationship.

The day before we went out into the wilderness, Jim had a precognition (we thought) of his mother's death, which caused us to talk at length and in detail about the meaning of death, our feelings about it, what kind of burial and requiem he felt were appropriate, etc. Thus, when I had to make those decisions about his death, I knew exactly how he would feel. And, oddly enough, he had "seen" his mother fall and felt that the fall might cause her death. I feel now it was a kind of premonition of his own manner of dying.

That same day, at lunch, Jim chose a title for his autobiography: *Nothing to Hide*. It was the first time I ever remember his considering an autobiography; he had always insisted it was "too early" for that. He outlined its content for me that day.

For months Jim's study and thought had more and more centered on the wilderness theme, and the depth of his response to the tradition centered there used to amaze me, even though in a more superficial way I felt its meaning too. So somehow our journey into the wilderness seemed—and seems—right to me. It is as though months had been spent in preparation for just what happened.

Yet we had no precognition at a conscious level of impending death, and for that I am very grateful. It meant that all our decisions were consistent with our over-all life-style. We had chosen to live our lives as fully as we could—being as open as possible to Life and all it could bring to us—so that we might grow as rapidly as we could toward the realization of our full human potential.

Each hour, each minute was spent living as fully as we knew how—searching for greater understanding, for Truth, through reading and research or through listening to and discussing with others; following our own desires and needs as we could detect them, trusting our bodies and spirits to guide us toward fulfillment; responding as fully as we could to the needs and desires of others;

enjoying, reflecting on, appreciating, pondering, evaluating, rejoicing in each experience in order to heighten our awareness and appreciation of life as it flooded in on us.

Such living in the fullness of the now leaves no time for calculating risks. It involves moving ahead in faith—trusting one's own potential and God's grace for the ability to respond—to be response-able in each new given moment.

Because of that style, which Jim and I consciously chose for our life together, we lived more deeply and had a larger variety of experiences in the span of our brief relationship than many people who live together for thirty or forty years, I feel sure. Our union was profound and complete. I wouldn't change that in the least.

But it was because of that same style that we set out by ourselves into the wilderness, making no provision for our own safety, not calculating the risk. Without changing all the rest, I could not have altered the end of the story. Therefore, I can have no regrets—I would not have wanted our life together to be any different.

There is a biblical story about Lot's wife (Genesis 19:15–26), whom God promised to save (along with her husband and their two daughters) from certain death in the destruction of Sodom. God's instructions to Lot had been: "Flee for your life; do not look back or stop anywhere in the valley; flee to the hills. . . ." But Lot's wife looked back, questioning, I'm sure, her decision to leave the security of her home for just a promise that she would be saved. The story says that she became a pillar of salt.

For me to look back would be an unworthy tribute to Jim—a man who lived so fully in the present and for the future. I have, as he did, much to learn from the past and I will treasure the memories of all I gained from, and the joy I knew in, my love and life with him. But there can be no regrets.

In the April issue of *Look* magazine (1969) we said: "And so with buoyant hearts, with a new 'believing hope' about a future not yet fully born, with the same beliefs we had before (not enough to suit some, too many to suit others), and with a renewed eagerness to minister to clergy and others in transition, we set forth on an unencumbered journey into an open future." I would not choose another life-style now, and I'm sure that a part of that open future for me involves learning to know and relate to Jim in a new way across or through what we usually think of as the barrier of death. I welcome that new experience which has already begun.

In that same *Look* article we quoted from the Qumrân *Manual of Discipline,* saying: "This is the time of clearing the way to go into the wilderness." We cleared the way, and went.

I do not intend to stop anywhere now in this valley of grief, but rather to walk steadily on to the hills, where new challenges and opportunities await me. I know God is there before me, and I step into that open future with faith that its meaning and promise will unfold before me.

I need not look back. There need be no pillars of salt— no regrets. Jim lives—and so do I.

*Peace and Joy.*